A WHO'S WHO OF WARWICKSHIRE COUNTY CRICKET CLUB

A Who's Who of

Robert
Brooke
and
David
Goodyear

Warwickshire County Cricket Club

ROBERT HALE · LONDON

© Robert Brooke and David Goodyear 1989
First published in Great Britain 1989

Robert Hale Limited
Clerkenwell House
Clerkenwell Green
London EC1R 0HT

British Library Cataloguing in Publication Data

Brooke, Robert
    A who's who of Warwickshire county cricket
    1. Warwickshire county cricket clubs
    Warwickshire county cricket club players to
    1988 – Biographies. Collections
    I. Title   II. Goodyear, David
    796,35′863′0922
ISBN 0–7090–3730-9

Photoset in North Wales by
Derek Doyle & Associates, Mold, Clwyd.
Printed in Great Britain by
St Edmundsbury Press Ltd, Bury St Edmunds, Suffolk.
Bound by WBC Bookbinders Limited.

Contents

Illustrations

In the process of writing this book, the authors have discovered a number of hitherto unseen portraits of Warwickshire players. The quality of photographs varies considerably, however, according to age and rarity, and it is hoped that readers will appreciate that reproduction has been difficult in some cases.

Half- and full-page illustrations are listed below.

In assembling a book of this nature it is difficult to trace all owners of original illustration material. If we have unintentionally failed to acknowledge any photographer, we would like to apologize and suggest that you contact us, care of our publishers.

R.B. & D.G.

Acknowledgements

The authors wish to thank the following for their help:

Mrs Frances Cartwright and staff, *Wolverhampton Express* and *Star*; the staff and management, *Birmingham Post* and *Mail* photograph library; the editor, *Birmingham Daily News*; Mr Patrick Baird, Birmingham Central Library (Local Studies); Mr Leslie Deakins and Ms Anne Courbet, Warwickshire Old Cricketers' Association; Warwickshire County Cricket Club; Mr John Reed; Mr John Taylor, Moseley Cricket Club; Mr Alex Davies; Mr Ken Lancaster, Aston Unity; Mr Clive Higgs; Mr John Reeve; Mr David Winslow; Brian Hunt. A special word of thanks must go to Mr Ken Kelly for allowing the usage of numerous photographs.

We are indebted to all relatives and friends of former players who have assisted with statistics and illustrations. Finally special thanks must go to the players themselves, without whom this book would not have been possible.

Foreword

by Peter Cranmer

This is a most interesting and comprehensive addition to Warwickshire history and to the roll of the present-day Old Players' Association, WOCCA. There are our giants, of course, and some whose names one hears occasionally from older members, of those who perhaps played once or twice. I played my first Second XI match at Stratford in 1928, and on the same ground forty years later – almost to the day – played my last. I was therefore lucky enough to know many of the giants – Frank Foster, Syd Santall, Jack Parsons, Crow Charlesworth, Willie Quaife, Bob Wyatt, Tiger Smith, Eric Hollies, Tom Dollery, Dennis Amiss, Mike Smith – and indeed played with most of them at various levels.

I have always respected Robert Brooke as a statistician, for anyone who can discover that I once took 7 for 52 for a Forces XI against H.E. the Governor of Bengal's XI on Eden Gardens, Calcutta, during the Second World War, must be a magician. It is right, too, that David Goodyear should be associated with this publication to join his book on Aston Villa; our two clubs have always been on friendly and co-operative terms and I remember that, as Warwickshire Captain, I was once allowed to address the Villa Park crowd at half-time to promote a Warwickshire Cricket Club membership drive.

The first time that I visited Edgbaston was in the early 1920s when my grandfather took me to see Middlesex; at the tea interval we went out to 'inspect the wicket' – little did I know then how often I should do just that before tossing the coin! It had been wet underfoot and I still recall trying to match the Warwickshire fast bowler Harry Howell's run-up marks. I wonder how many present-day youngsters will remember doing the same with Bob Willis and Gladstone Small in sixty or seventy years' time. This book brings back a host of memories for me, as I am sure it will for Warwickshire supporters and cricket enthusiasts everywhere.

Introduction

A Short History

Neither by tradition nor adoption is cricket regarded as natural to Warwickshire yet the game has in fact flourished within the county for more than two centuries.

As long ago as 1760 the landlord of the Bell Inn, Smallbrook Street, Birmingham ran a 'cricket society' (team) and his advertisement for matches in *Aris' Birmingham Gazette* on 14 July 1760 is the first-known press mention of the game in Warwickshire. The early years of the nineteenth century saw the game thriving in the rural areas and in 1826 the Wellbourne (or Wellesbourne) Cricket Club decided to reconstitute itself as 'Warwickshire Cricket Club' with a ground adjacent to the racecourse at Warwick. No matches can be traced as having been played by this 'County' Club; it shortly returned to Wellesbourne village and the first game known to have been advertised and played as a Warwickshire County match took place in Coventry on 7 and 8 August 1843, Warwickshire defeating Leicestershire by 8 wickets. As no county club existed this could not possibly be regarded as an 'official' inter-county contest but players, press and spectators all appear to have regarded it as such, and one feels that contemporary opinion is more relevant than the niceties of 'officialdom'.

Another 'Warwickshire County Cricket Club' was formed in 1864, with headquarters at Warwick but although playing a number of matches during the next few years it was in no way representative of cricket throughout the county. The playing personnel consisted almost wholly of 'gentry' and the heavily populated industrial area of Birmingham was ignored. County cricket was now developing apace throughout the country and Warwickshire was being left behind and in March 1882 the Warwickshire Gentlemen's Club organised an unofficial gathering of interested parties from various areas, including Birmingham. There was general agreement on the idea of a broadly based county club and a few weeks later, at the Queen's Hotel, Coventry, the Warwickshire County Cricket Club was officially formed.

Matters were to run far from smoothly; in the following year a despairing William Ansell, secretary of the Birmingham Cricket Association, complained that the 'gentlemen's' Club was still playing under the county label, but this difficulty removed itself at the end of

1883 with the demise of the Warwick Club. The opportunity then presented itself for the County Club to strengthen its base throughout the county. Discussions with regard to a fixed ground were commenced in 1884 and, although the rural lobby was still strong in its prejudice against Birmingham, by 1886 it had been accepted that this was the only possible location and the ground on the Calthorpe Estate at Edgbaston was acquired and opened.

Progress in the following years was steady. William Ansell, now Honorary Secretary, recognised that the Club was still below par with regard to playing strength and so he set out to attract professionals, with the ultimate aim of Warwickshire's being accepted into the top echelons of county cricket. After a number of disappointments the county was finally granted first-class status, but outside the County Championship, in 1894, and the following season Ansell's final ambition was realised and Warwickshire gained entry into the official County Championship.

This emergence had to be seen as a beginning to be worked on, rather than an end. Three professional bowlers – Jack Shilton, Harry Pallett and Jim Whitehead – had done most to secure promotion but by 1895 for various reasons each was past his best, while despite the valuable batting of professional imports like Walter Quaife and Teddy Diver, and the enormous promise of Walter's young brother and ex-Sussex Colt, Billy, it was seen as vital that new talent be unearthed and nurtured. Fortunately, around the turn of the century fine bowlers such as Syd Santall (medium), Frank Field (fast) and Sam Hargreave, a left-armed spinner from Lancashire, began to make their mark, while Billy Quaife's heavy scoring was supplemented by the emergence of left-hander Sep Kinneir from Wiltshire, Jack Devey, celebrated Soccer player and tyro baseball star, and Yorkshireman Crowther Charlesworth. Also, 'Dick' Lilley, with the club from pre-first-class days, had developed into the finest wicketkeeper-batsman in the *world*.

Another important milestone in the advance of Warwickshire cricket was the allocation of an Australian Test in 1902. Manifestly the importance of Warwickshire, and Birmingham, in the cricket world was now recognised in high places but on the field the county seemed to get into a rut. Amidst several captaincy changes mid-table seemed the limit of Warwickshire's playing ambitions but this all changed in 1911 with the stroke of genius which persuaded the committee to offer the captaincy to the 22-old F.R. Foster.

Foster, an enormously promising left-armed pace bowler and mid-order batsman, transformed the playing fortunes immediately, and in his first season Warwickshire became County Champions for the first time. Foster himself topped both sets of Championship averages but his personal miracle could not have been performed without the support of stalwart bowlers Field (122 wickets) and Santall, the batting of Quaife, Kinneir and Charlesworth, and the outstanding wicket-keeping of the emergent 'Tiger' Smith. The county's triumph was greeted with great enthusiasm but any hopes that form would be maintained in 1912 were soon dashed. After a good start the county sank to ninth position and there was little improvement before the Kaiser ended county cricket for five years.

Great changes had been wrought when the County Championship resumed in 1919, and for Warwickshire the most important loss was that of Frank Foster. Injuries in a wartime road accident prevented him from resuming his career, though realistically, other health problems were showing themselves and these may have prevented his return even had he remained physically able. Kinneir and Santall also failed to re-appear; promising paceman Percy Jeeves had died on the French battlefields; Jack Parsons remained with the military in India; while Field and Billy Quaife, in their mid-forties, were shadows of their former selves.

In 1919 last place was attained for the first time and the 1920s were notable only for consistent mediocrity. The Hon. F.S.G. Calthorpe, talented all-rounder, was too gentlemanly to make a successful captain while the batting, led by R.E.S. Wyatt and dour Yorkshireman Norman Kilner was usually prolific but scored runs at insufficient pace. Lion-hearted Harry Howell, local and really fast, carried the bowling which otherwise was woefully inadequate.

Signs of improvement were manifest in the early 1930s. Wyatt, the heaviest scorer since the heyday of Quaife became skipper and the arrival of left-armed spinner George Paine and gallant seamer Danny Mayer injected some much-needed penetration and stamina into an attack previously short on both these attributes. Most important, two players whose influence for good was to be at the forefront of Warwickshire cricket for a quarter of a century made their debuts. The comfortably built Black Country leg-spinner Eric Hollies started in 1932 and two years later he was joined by H.E. ('Tom') Dollery, an infinitely promising batsman from Berkshire.

Regrettably the team never really gelled under Wyatt and for 1938, amidst all sorts of recrimination, he was replaced by the enthusiastic but inexperienced Peter Cranmer. Wyatt stayed with the Club until the outbreak of war but left in 1946 to join local rivals, Worcestershire. Relieving Wyatt of the captaincy failed to have the desired effect, and from a distance of forty years one feels that the troubles were more deep-seated. Santall's years as coach had produced little in the shape of local talent while there were murmurings that some players were given better treatment than others. Reg Santall, despite inconsistency and indiscipline, seemed guaranteed a place, yet the cultured Aubrey Hill was allowed few failures before his place was in jeopardy.

Much rebuilding was required when cricket resumed in 1946. Cranmer remained as captain, while Dollery and Hollies were now genuine Test material, but Anno Domini accounted for a number of pre-war stalwarts while George Paine found that arthritis had destroyed his action and his ability to bowl long spells.

Cranmer relinquished the captaincy after the 1947 season, Dollery and the Oxford amateur R.H. Maudsley taking over as joint skippers, an unsatisfactory arrangement which lasted one season only and with Maudsley's agreement Dollery became the first Warwickshire professional to be appointed sole captain, in 1949. The effect was electrifying; playing positive and entertaining cricket the county occupied fourth place in 1949 and 1950 and then in 1951 they won the title for the second time.

Dollery was a marvellous captain; he gave his players a cheerful confidence in their own abilities while, apart from his own tactical awareness, he scored more than 1500 runs, usually when most needed, and set a fine example in the field. Not that it was a one-man team; left-handed Dick Spooner kept wicket well, and with 1700 runs made an ideal opening partner for the solid Fred Gardner. Wolton and Ord scored valuably in the middle order while all-rounder Alan Townsend was an admirable 'bits-and-pieces' player and the best close field in the country. Eric Hollies, the bedrock of the bowling, took 145 wickets, receiving admirable support from pacemen Tom Pritchard and Charlie Grove, and young left-arm spinner Ray Weeks.

Sadly, the decline soon set in; it became apparent that those who had carried the side since the war would need replacing. Dollery retired after 1955 and two years later Hollies marked his own last season with 128 wickets. Despite the valiant coaching efforts of 'Tiger' Smith and the West Indian, Derief Taylor, the county's efforts at finding new talent were not invariably successful, but *all* was not gloom and despair.

Under the inspiration of Club Secretary Leslie Deakins, the 1950s marked the development of Edgbaston into one of the best equipped arenas in the country, and in 1957 came the long-awaited return of Test cricket to Birmingham.

On the playing side, the 1950s saw the arrival of some talented performers, though in insufficient numbers to produce another Championship. Jack Bannister was a high-quality seamer, later to become a respected journalist, and Jim Stewart hit the ball harder than most until the injury bug butted in. Tom Cartwright was a talented all-rounder while M.J.K. Smith, signed from Leicestershire, began a long stint of service as batsman, captain and committeeman.

Problems over Spooner's wicketkeeping replacement were solved when A.C. Smith came down from Oxford in 1960 and he was to prove a natural successor to Mike Smith as captain and, in 1975, to Leslie Deakins as General Secretary. David Brown arrived as an effective and enthusiastic pace bowler while Billy Ibadulla succeeded Townsend in the utility spot, but the most notable arrival in the early 1960s was undoubtedly Dennis Amiss.

Taken on the staff in 1958 after an outstanding schoolboy record, he first played as a 17-year-old all-rounder in 1960, becoming a regular in 1965 after back trouble had killed his seam bowling. His contributions fluctuated somewhat until 1972 when he moved up to opener, assimilating his new role as to the manner born. It is well-known history that when Amiss retired in 1987 he had scored more runs and hundreds for Warwickshire than any other player, had obtained 102 centuries in all, and won 50 England caps.

Amiss's opening partner throughout much of the 1970s was John Jameson, a popular member of the club who enjoyed taking the game to the bowlers and regularly flayed the medium pacers (those supposedly too negative to attack!). The transfusion of four talented West Indians, Rohan Kanhai, Lance Gibbs, Alvin Kallicharran and Deryck Murray into an already useful side under the astute Alan Smith signalled a determined championship bid. They were runners-up in 1971 and went one better the following season.

The 1972 title marked the end of another era. Most of the subsequent period has seen Warwickshire languishing in the lower reaches of the Championship, only the occasional limited overs successes having brought relief, and despite frequent changes of leadership the decline showed little sign of being reversed. David Brown was a popular successor to A.C. Smith as captain, but enjoyed little success, while John Whitehouse was unfortunate in that his two seasons of captaincy coincided with the Kerry Packer 'troubles'. The appointment in 1980 of Bob Willis as skipper, and David Brown first ever cricket manager, merely accelerated the decline as far as the Championship was concerned and the depths were reached with last place in both 1981 and 1982.

A temporary improvement coincided with the arrival from Worcestershire of experienced left-arm spinner Norman Gifford but the three years from 1985 saw another collapse in on-field performances and, seemingly, morale. Gifford resigned the captaincy in 1987 after three troubled seasons and, after a special general meeting in November 1987 saw the committee narrowly win a vote of confidence, manager David Brown was relieved of his responsibilities. A new manager was appointed – ex-Hants and Northants bowler Bob Cottam – and opening bat Andy Lloyd was made captain.

This gifted left-hander had largely regained confidence after a horrific head injury on his Test debut in 1984. His first season in the captaincy saw a big improvement in the fortunes of the county and he batted with a new assurance on some often-indifferent Edgbaston wickets.

Although his batting deserted him in 1988, Geoff Humpage's record suggested that he was the best county batsman-wicketkeeper since the great Leslie Ames; chunky Andy Moles, a late developer, shows possibilities of many years' heavy scoring, while Birmingham-reared Asif Din belatedly established himself as a stylish no. 3. The talented Paul Smith had a number of disappointments to put behind him, but still had great, unfulfilled, potential as a high-order batsman and lively bowler. Gladstone Small promised to spearhead the bowling for several years to come, and had lively new ball partners in Tony Merrick or Alan Donald. Tim Munton seemed likely to make the grade as support seamer but the development of a spinner was a matter of urgency. Several years of the largest and most experienced coaching staff in the Club's history had left the cupboard bare.

With long-serving Alvin Kallicharran now a 'home' player – though aged 40 he could hardly be anything other than a short-term asset – the team seemed generally stronger than for many years. There was cautious optimism for the immediate future, and great hopes in the longer term.

Glossary

LB	leg-break bowler
LBG	leg-break and googly bowler
LFM	left-armed fast-medium bowler
LHB	left-handed batsman
North W	North Warwickshire
OB	off-break bowler
RAS	right-armed spin bowler
RF	right-armed fast bowler
RFM	right-armed fast-medium bowler
RHB	right-handed batsman
RM	right-armed medium-paced bowler
SLA	left-armed slow bowler
U	University
W	Warwickshire
WCCC	Warwickshire County Cricket Club
WK	Wicketkeeper
*	not out

Notes on statistics

Debut + year	Season of first-class debut for Warwickshire
Cap + year	Year of award of county cap
Benefit + amount + date	Season of benefit match and amount of money obtained

All details on cricket performances are for first-class matches unless otherwise stated.

Where no county is given after place of birth or death it can be taken as Warwickshire.

ABBERLEY, Robert Neal – RHB RM
b. Birmingham, 22 April 1944. Educated at Saltley Grammar School, Birmingham.

Debut 1964 v Cambridge U, Cambridge. 258 matches for W 1964–79 (cap 1966). Benefit (£39,752) 1979. Highest score: W 117* v Essex, Edgbaston 1966. Best bowling: W 2–19 v Oxford U, The Parks 1972. 1000 runs (3); 1281 (29.11) 1966 best.

County Chief Coach since 1981. Toured Pakistan with England under-25s 1966–67 (returned early due to injury). Full first-class record: 10082 runs (24.47); 5 wickets (58.80).

ABELL, Roy Beverley – RHB LB
b. Birmingham, 21 January 1931. Educated at Waverley Grammar School, Birmingham.

Debut 1967 v Cambridge U, Edgbaston.

1 match for W 1967. Did not bat. Best bowling: W 3–64 in only match.

Played for Moseley in Birmingham League.

He is a professional artist who was commissioned by Her Majesty The Queen for a Silver Jubilee picture. Illustrated club grounds in *First in the Field*, by Alex E. Davies (1988), a history of the Birmingham and District Cricket League.

ADDERLEY, Charles Henry – RHB RM
b. King's Heath, Birmingham, 16 September 1912; d. Moseley, Birmingham, 28 February 1985. Educated at Moseley College.

Debut 1946 v Sussex, Edgbaston. 5 matches for W 1946 (amateur). Highest score 12 v Notts., Trent Bridge 1946. Best bowling: W 1–19 v Notts., Trent Bridge

1946.
Played club cricket for King's Heath for many years; also appeared for Moseley in Birmingham League.

ALLAN, James Moffat – RHB SLA
b. Leeds, Yorkshire, 2 April 1932. Educated at Edinburgh Academy and Worcester College, Oxford.

Debut v Leics., Nuneaton 1966. 48 matches for W 1966-68. Highest score: W 76* v Sussex, Hove 1967. Best bowling: W 5–11 v Sussex, Edgbaston 1967.

First-class debut for Oxford U 1953; won Oxford Blue 1953-56. 39 matches for Scotland 1954–72; 40 matches for Kent 1954–57 (cap 1955). Highest first-class score: 153, Oxford U v Sussex, Oxford 1953. Best first-class bowling 7–54, Scotland v Pakistanis, Selkirk 1971. Scored 121* and 105 in same match, Kent v Northants, Northampton 1955.

AMISS, Dennis Leslie – RHB LM/SLA
b. Harborne, Birmingham, 7 April 1943. Educated at Oldknow Road School, Small Heath, Birmingham.

Debut 1960 v Surrey, The Oval, as a professional. 547 matches for W 1960–87 (cap 1965). Benefit (£34,947) 1975; testimonial (£85,000) 1985. Highest score: W 232* v Glos., Bristol 1979. Best bowling: W 3–21 v Middlesex, Lord's 1970. 1000 runs (20) 1965–87 (equalling W's record held by W.G. Quaife). 2030 (53.42) 1978 best. 35146 runs (41.64) for W – the county record; 78 centuries for the county (another record). Scored a century and

Dennis Amiss, Warwickshire's highest-scoring batsman

more than 1000 runs for W against every other county.

50 Tests for England 1966–77: 3612 runs (46.30), 11 centuries; highest score: 262* v West Indies, Kingston 1973–74. 1379 Test runs in 1974 – best in calendar year for England. 43423 runs (42.86) in first-class career; 102 first-class centuries. Played early cricket for Smethwick (Birmingham League).

Autobiography: *In Search of Runs* (1976). Awarded MBE in 1988 New Years Honours.

ASIF DIN, Mohamed ('Gunga') – RHB LB
b. Kampala, Uganda, 21 September 1960. Educated at Ladywood Comprehensive School.

Debut 1981 v Yorks. Edgbaston. 141 matches for W 1981-88 (cap 1987). Highest

score: W 158* v Cambridge U, Cambridge 1988. Best Bowling: W 5–100 v Glam., Edgbaston 1982. 1000 Runs (2); 1425 (38.51) 1988 best.

AUSTIN, Harry – LHB SLA
b. Moseley, Birmingham, 17 April 1892; d. Canterbury, Kent, 28 August 1968.

Debut 1919 v Surrey, The Oval. 4 matches for W 1919 (professional). Highest score: W 13 v Yorks., Edgbaston 1919. Best bowling: W 1–47 v Surrey, The Oval 1919 (on debut).

Played two matches for Worcs. 1928. Professional for Kidderminster in Birmingham League; later cricket coach and groundsman.

BAKER, Charles Shaw – LHB LB
b. Moss Side, Manchester, 5 January 1883,
d. Lehant, Corn., 16 December 1976.
Educated at Hulme Grammar School,
Manchester.

Debut 1905 v Somerset, Edgbaston. 214
matches for W 1905-20 (professional – cap
1906). Highest score: W 155* v Worcs.,
Worcester 1910. Best bowling: 4–59 v
Lancs., Edgbaston 1912. 1000 runs (3);
1242 (33.56) 1913 best.

Added 199 with A.F.A. Lilley v Surrey,
The Oval 1906; then county 6th-wicket
record. Played club cricket for Leamington
before W debut; later played as amateur
for Corn., captain 1925–30.

Also played soccer for Aston Villa.
Became well known as a cartoonist in
national newspapers and cricket
publications; also as 'lightning artist' on
music halls.

BAINBRIDGE, Herbert William – RHB
Round arm RH change bowler.
b. Gowhatti, Assam, India, 29 October
1862, d. Leamington Spa, 3 April 1940.
Educated at Eton College and Cambridge
U.

Debut 1894 v Notts., Trent Bridge.
(First-class debut – had played for county
since 1886; first match v Australia, before
he was qualified.) 118 matches for W
1894–1902 (amateur). County Captain
1887–1901. Highest score: W 162 v Hants,
Southampton 1897. Best bowling: W 1–5 v
Derby. Edgbaston 1900. 1000 runs (2)
1895–96.

Played 11 matches for Surrey 1883–85;
Cambridge Blue 1884–86. W Hon
Secretary 1903–40; Chairman 1931–39.
Played club cricket for Leamington.

H.W. Bainbridge was Warwickshire's first captain in first-class cricket. He also served as honorary secretary (1903–40) and chairman (1931–39)

BANKS, David Andrew – RHB RM
b. Pensnett, Staffs., 11 January 1961.
Educated at Pensnett Secondary Sch.,
Dudley Technical College.

Debut 1988, v Worcs., Edgbaston. 7
Matches for W 1988. Highest score: W 61 v
Sri Lanka, Edgbaston 1988.

19 matches for Worcs., 1983–85, scoring
100 and 53 on debut, v Oxford U, Oxford.
Played for Staffs. 1986–88. Has played in
Birmingham League for Old Hill,
Stourbridge, West Bromwich and
Dartmouth.

**BANNISTER, John David ('Jack') – RHB
RFM**
b. Wolverhampton, 23 August 1930.
Educated at King Edward's Grammar
School, Five Ways, Birmingham.

Debut 1950 v Glam. Swansea. 368
matches for W 1950–68 (professional – cap
1954). Benefit (£8,846) 1964. Highest
score: W 71 v Derbys., Nuneaton (Griff
and Coton) 1960. Best bowling: W 10–41 v
Combined Services, Portland Road 1959.
100 wickets (3) 131 (21.21) 1961 best.

Played Birmingham League Cricket for
Mitchell's & Butlers. A back injury during
the late 1950s caused him to adjust his

action, without affecting his bowling
success.

A Walsall bookmaker, cricket reporter
for the *Birmingham Post*, journalist for
Wisden Cricket Monthly, and commentator
on radio and BBC Television. Cricketers'
Association Chairman 1968–69; Secretary
since 1970.

BARBER, Eric George – RHB
b. Bishopsgate Green, Coventry, 22 July
1915.

Debut 1936 v Derby., Edgbaston. 2 matches for W 1936 (professional). Highest score: W 13 on debut.

Played as professional in Coventry League.

BARBER, Robert William – LHB RALBG
b. Withington, Manchester, 26 September 1935. Educated at Ruthin, Magdalene College, Cambridge.

Debut 1963 v Hants, Courtaulds 1963. 124 matches for W 1963–69 (cap 1963). Highest score: W 138 v Australia, Edgbaston 1964 (scored before lunch on first morning). Best bowling: W 6–74 v Derby., Edgbaston 1963. Performed hat trick, W v Glam., Edgbaston 1963. One of longest and most accurate throwers to play for W.

First-class debut Lancs. 1954; 156 matches Lancs. 1954–62 (cap 1958 –

captain 1960–61). Played for Cambridge U 1955–57, Blue 1956–57. 28 Tests for England 1960–68; 1495 runs (35.59); 42 wickets (43.00). Highest score: 185 v Australia, Sydney 1965–66. 17631 runs (29.43), 549 wickets (29.46) in first-class career.

Is MCC honorary member.

BARBER, William Henry – RHB RFM
b. Nuneaton, 23 July 1906; d. Coventry, 13 January 1980. Educated at Chilvers Coton C. of E. School.

Debut 1927 v Notts., Edgbaston. 5 matches for W 1927–33 (professional). Highest score: W 23 v Worcs., Dudley

1933. Best bowling: W 3–81 v Glam., Edgbaston 1933.

Professional for Nuneaton and for various northern clubs; also played for Cheshire.

BARBERY, Alfred Edward – RHB RFM
b. Marylebone, London, 13 October 1884; d. Solihull, 23 May 1973.

Debut 1906 v Surrey, Edgbaston. 2 matches for W 1906–07 (professional). Highest score: W 6 v Surrey, Edgbaston 1906. Best bowling: W 2–64 v S. Africa,

Edgbaston 1907. First W professional to play in spectacles.

Was professional and groundsman, Leamington CC.

BARKER, Maurice Percy – RHB RMF
b. Leamington Spa, 4 February 1917.

Debut 1946 v Sussex, Edgbaston. 5 Matches for W 1946 (amateur). Highest score: W 17 v Sussex, Hove 1946. Best bowling: W 7–68 v Yorks., Edgbaston 1946.

Played for Leamington from age 15.
Was a police officer, W Constabulary.

BARNES, Terry Peter – RHB WK
b. Coventry, 13 November 1933. Educated at King Henry VIII School, Coventry.

Debut 1956 v Scotland, Edgbaston (only match; professional). Highest score: W 7.

Played club cricket for Kenilworth.

BARNES, Sydney Francis – RHB Versatile RFM.
b. Smethwick, Staffs., 19 April 1873; d. Chadsmoor, Staffs., 26 December 1967.

Debut 1894 v Glos., Clifton College. 4 matches for W 1894–96 (professional). Highest score: W 18 v Essex, Leyton 1896. Best bowling: W 2–95 v Surrey, The Oval 1895.

46 matches for Lancashire 1899–1903; played 1927–30 for Wales. 27 Tests for England 1901–02 to 1913–14; 242 runs (8.06) and 189 wickets (16.43). Took 9–103 v S. Africa, Jo'burg 1913–14 and 49 wickets (10.93) in the series – still a record.

In first-class cricket took 719 wickets (17.09) and scored 1573 runs (12.78), but most of career was spent with his native Staffs. (1904–34 with gaps) and in League cricket in which he had unrivalled reputation. At age 55 took 76 wickets (8.21) for Staffs. Signed final professional contract aged 65.

An original Hon. member of MCC in 1949. Regarded as one of the greatest bowlers of all-time.

BARTON, Joseph – RHB RF
Probably b. Hitcham, near Lavenham, Suffolk, 13 March 1859;[1] d. Selly Oak, Birmingham, 31 January 1945.

Debut 1895 v Essex, Edgbaston. 3 matches for W 1895–96 (professional; also played non-first-class for W 1894). Highest score: W 16 v Surrey, Edgbaston 1896. Best bowling: W 5–73 on debut.

Also played for Staffs., and Birmingham League for Handsworth Wood, where he was professional and groundsman. Later he was groundsman at Olton Golf Club.

[1] It has proved impossible to be certain of Barton's birthplace and date. The above details seem likely to be correct, but he could also be the Joseph Barton born at Allesley, W on 17 January 1859.

BATES, Leonard Thomas Ashton – RHB SRA
b. Edgbaston Cricket Ground, 20 March 1895; d. Coldwaltham, Sussex, 11 March 1971. Educated at Tindall Street School.

Debut 1913 v Sussex, The Butts, Coventry. 440 matches for W 1913–35 (professional – cap 1919). Benefit (£792) 1930. Highest score; W 211 v Glos., Gloucester 1932. Best bowling: 2–16 v Middlesex, Lord's 1926. 1000 runs (12); 1518 (33.73) 1926 best.

Scored 116 and 144 v Kent, Coventry Butts 1927. Twice carried bat throughout an innings; 96 out of 207 v Surrey, The Oval 1921 and 50 out of 125 v Yorks. Huddersfield 1922.

Played for Aston Unity in Birmingham League and after retirement became Coach at Christ's Hospital, Horsham. Father John Bates was groundsman at Edgbaston and brother S.H. Bates played for W. Son-in-law D.J. Weekes played for Sussex 1952.

BATES, Samuel Harold – RHB SLA
b. Edgbaston Cricket Ground, 16 June 1890; d. in action near Hardecourt, France, 28 August 1916. Educated at Tindall Street School.

Debut 1910 v Leics., Leicester. 5 matches for W 1910–12 (professional). Highest score for W 13 v Middlesex, Edgbaston 1912. Best bowling for W 3–56 v Surrey, The Oval 1911.

Father John Bates was groundsman at Edgbaston and brother L.T.A. Bates played for W.

BENJAMIN, Harold Lewis – RHB RFM
b. St Thomas Parish, Birmingham, 13 April 1892; d. Tettenhall, Staffs., 7 August 1942.

Debut 1919 v Yorks. Edgbaston. 2 matches for W 1919 (amateur). Highest score: W 23 v Worcs., Edgbaston 1919. Best bowling: W 1–48 same match.

1 match for Northants 1928.

BAYLEY, Martin George – RHB SLA
b. Leamington Spa, 10 July 1952. Educated at Campion High School, Leamington Spa.

Debut 1969 v Cambridge U, Edgbaston (aged 16). 2 matches for W 1969. Highest score for W 1* on debut. Best bowling: W 2–54 v Scotland, Edgbaston 1969.

Played club cricket for A.P. Leamington.

BAYNTON, Robert Geoffrey – RHB LM
b. Moseley, Birmingham, 5 March 1900; d. in road accident, King's Heath, Birmingham, 26 August 1924.

Debut 1921 v Som., Edgbaston. 13 matches for W 1921–23 (amateur). Highest score: W 36 v Lancs., Edgbaston 1922. Best bowling: W 4–56 v Notts., Edgbaston 1922.

Played for Moseley in Birmingham League.

BENJAMIN, Joseph Emmanuel ('Joey') – RHB RFM
b. St Kitts, West Indies, 2 February 1961.

Educated at Cayon High School, St Kitts; Mount Pleasant School, Highgate, Birmingham.

Debut 1988 v Sri Lanka, Edgbaston (only match).

Played for Staffs. in 1986–88 and for Dudley and Mitchells & Butlers in the Birmingham League.

BENSON, Gwynfor Leonard – RHB OB
b. Birmingham, 7 January 1941. Educated at Coleshill Grammar School.

Debut 1959 v Scotland, Edgbaston. 3 matches for W 1959–61 (amateur). Highest score: W 46 v Cambridge U, Portland Road 1961.

Played for Birmingham League cricket for Smethwick. Hockey for W and Wales.

BLENKIRON, William – RHB RFM
b. Newfield Estate, Bishop Auckland, Co.

Durham, 21 July 1942.

Debut 1964 v Scotland, Edgbaston. 117 matches for W 1964–74 (cap 1969). Highest score: W 62 v Worcs., Dudley 1969. Best bowling: W 5–37 v Leics., Leicester 1968.

Played for Durham County 1975–76 and in club cricket in Durham.

BOURNE, William Anderson – RHB RFM
b. Clapham St Michael, Barbados, 15 November 1952. Educated at Harrison College, Barbados.

Debut 1973 v Oxford U, Edgbaston. 59 matches for W 1973–77. Highest score: W 107 v Sussex, Edgbaston 1976. Best bowling: W 6–47 v Cambridge U, Edgbaston 1976.

First-class debut for Barbados 1970–71. Played in Moin-ud-Dowlah Tournament in India and represented East Africa in World Cup. Also played for Zambia, and lately coach and cricket writer in Zimbabwe. Played in Birmingham League for West Bromwich Dartmouth.

BREEDEN, Carl Louis – RHB RM
b. Moseley, Birmingham, 10 February 1891; d. Claverdon, W, 2 November 1951. Educated at King Edward's School, Birmingham.
Debut 1910 v Yorks., Huddersfield. 5 matches for W 1910 (amateur). Highest score: W 27 v Leics., Leicester 1910.
Frank Breeden (uncle) played W 1883–87. Played in Birmingham League for Moseley.

BREWSTER, Vincent Crescedo – LHB SLA
b. Bridgetown, Barbados, 2 January 1940.
Debut 1965 v Oxford U, Edgbaston. 2 matches for W 1965. Highest score: W 35* on debut. Best bowling: W 7–58 same match.
Became professional with Norton in 1966; subsequently played for Addiscombe (Surrey).

BRIDGE, Walter Basil – RHB OB
b. Birmingham, 29 May 1938.
Debut 1955 v Glam., Neath. 98 matches for W 1955–68 (professional – cap 1961). Highest score: W 56* v Indians, Edgbaston 1959. Best bowling: W 8–56 v Cambridge U, Edgbaston 1959. 100 wickets (1) 121 (22.75) 1961.
Played club cricket for Pickwick and Studley. County career curtailed by injury and illness.

BRINDLE, Reginald Gordon – RHB
b. Warrington, Cheshire, 3 October 1925
Debut 1949 v Combined Services, Edgbaston (only match) (professional). Highest score: W 42.

BROBERG, Ralph Francis – LHB SLA
b. Balsall Heath, Birmingham, 21 July 1899; d. Hall Green, Birmingham, 3 September 1938. Educated at King Edward's Grammar School, Camp Hill, Birmingham.

Debut 1920 v Som., Edgbaston (only match – amateur). Scored 4 in only innings.

Played club cricket for Olton and King's Heath.

English Schoolboy Rugby Union International; played club rugby for Moseley.

BROMLEY, Philip Harry – RHB OB
b. Stratford-upon-Avon, 30 July 1930. Educated at Warwick School.

Debut 1947 v Scotland, Edgbaston. 49 matches for W 1947–56 (professional until 1956). Highest score: W 121* v Essex, Edgbaston 1952. Best bowling: W 5–61 v Worcs., Worcester 1953.

Played for Shrops. 1958–70; Birmingham League Cricket for Moseley; also played for Knowle, & Dorridge and Leamington.

BROWN, Albert – RHB RFM
b. Birmingham, 29 July 1911.

Debut 1932 v India, Edgbaston (only match – amateur). Highest score: W 1*. Best bowling: W 2–61.

Played for Cannon Hill CC (Birmingham Parks).

Was a top class billiards and snooker player.

BROWN, David John – RHB RFM
b. Walsall, Staffs., 30 January 1942. Educated at Queen Mary Grammar School, Walsall.

Debut 1961 v Scotland, Edgbaston. 325 matches for W 1961–82 (professional) (cap 1964 – captain 1975–77). Benefit (£21,109) 1973. Highest score: W 79 v Derby., Edgbaston 1972. Best bowling: W 8–60 v Middlesex, Lord's 1975. Was first cricket manager of W 1980–87.

26 Tests for England 1965–69. 342 runs (11.79) 79 wickets (28.31). Best Test bowling 5–42 v Australia, Lord's 1968. 1165 wickets (24.85) in first-class career. Birmingham League for Walsall.

Is a well-known breeder of racehorses and greyhounds.

BROWN, Edward – RHB RFM
b. Newcastle-on-Tyne, 27 November 1911;
d. Birmingham, 14 April 1978. Educated at Darlington Grammar School.

Debut 1932 v Glam., Edgbaston. 28 matches for W 1932–34 (professional) (cap 1933). Highest score: W 19* v Sussex, Edgbaston 1933. Best bowling: W 8–35 v Surrey, Edgbaston 1933.

Also played County cricket for Northumb. and Durham and his clubs include West Bromwich Dartmouth (Birmingham League) and Darlington.

Soccer for Sevette FC (Switzerland).

BROWN, John Dowell – LHB SLA
b. Coventry, 25 August 1890; d. Leamington Spa, 18 March 1968.

Debut 1913 v Worcs., Dudley. 9 matches for W 1913–14. (professional). Highest score: W 7 v Yorks., Sheffield 1913. Best bowling: W 4–18 v Worcs., Dudley 1913 (on debut).

Played club cricket for Leamington.

BUCKINGHAM, John ('Jack', 'Buck', 'The Duke') – RHB WK
b. Grimethorpe, Yorks., 21 January 1903.
d. Moseley, Birmingham, 25 January 1987. Educated at Grimethorpe School.

Debut 1933 v West Indies, Edgbaston. 93 matches for W 1933–39 (professional – cap 1937). Highest score: W 137* v Northants, Northampton 1938. 1000 runs (1); 1054 (31.00) 1938 best. Added 220 with Tom Dollery v Derby., Derby 1938; 6th wicket record for the county. Dismissed 4 batsmen 'stumped' in an innings, v Surrey, The Oval 1938 – still the record for the county.

Coach at Wellesbourne School after retirement; also sports reporter for local newspapers, umpire and soccer referee.

BULPITT, Neville John – RHB RM
b. Coventry, 15 April 1957. Educated at Caludon Castle School, Coventry.

Played only three times for W in Sunday League 1979.

Plays for Coventry Highway CC in Coventry League.

BURTON, Reginald Henry Markham RHB
b. Leamington Spa, 23 March 1900; d. Rugby, 19 October 1980. Educated at

Lawrence Sheriff School, Rugby.
Debut 1919 v Worcs., Worcester (only match – amateur). Highest score: W 47 in only innings.

Played for Rugby CC; Captain 1928–47, President 1950–80.

BUSHER, Harold Aston – RHB
b. Sparkhill, Birmingham, 2 August 1876; d. in Australia, October 1954.

Debut 1908 v Glos., Edgbaston (only match – amateur). Highest score: W 15.

Played for Barnes CC (London); appeared for Suffolk 1913–14.

Brother, S.E. Busher, played for Worcs. and Surrey.

BYRNE, George Robert – RHB RM
b. Northfield, Birmingham, 28 May 1892. d. Torteval, Guernsey, 23 June 1973. Educated at Downside.

Debut 1912 v Middlesex, Edgbaston. 8 matches for W 1912 (amateur). Highest score: W 11 v Hants, Bournemouth 1912. Best bowling: W 3–9 v Middx., Edgbaston 1912 (on debut) (took 3 wickets in 4 balls).

4 matches for Worcs 1914–21. Played for Moseley in Birmingham League.

Uncle, J.F. Byrne, played for Warwickshire.

BYRNE, James Frederick – RHB RFM
b. Penns, near Birmingham, 19 June 1871;

M.J.F. Byrne, captain (1903–07]

d. Edgbaston, 10 May 1954. Educated at Downside.

Debut 1897 v Leics., Edgbaston (played non-first-class since 1892). 138 matches for W 1897–1912 (amateur). Captain 1903–06; Joint Captain (with T.S. Fishwick) 1907. Highest score: W 222 v Lancashire, Edgbaston 1905. Scored 100 v Leics.,

Edgbaston 1897 on first-class debut. Best bowling: W 5–37 v Leics., Leicester 1904. Added 333 with S. Kinneir v Lancs., Edgbaston 1905 – W record for 1st wicket until 1960.

Played in Birmingham League for Moseley.

Played Rugby Union Football for Moseley and England (Captain 1897–98). Nephew, G.R. Byrne, played for W and Worcs.

CANNINGS, Victor Henry Douglas – RHB RM

b. Bighton, Hants., 3 April 1919; Educated at Guildford Technical College.

Debut 1947 v Northants, Northampton. 53 matches for W 1947–49 (professional – cap 1947). Highest score: W 61 v Notts., Edgbaston 1947. Best bowling: W 5–49 v Sussex, Hove 1947.

Played 230 for matches Hants 1950–59; cap 1950; benefit (£3,188) 1959. Best bowling in first-class cricket 7–52, Hants v Oxford U, Oxford 1950. 100 wickets in season 4 times for Hants. Took 927 wickets (22.73) in first-class career. Played for Bucks 1960–62.

Coach at Eton since 1960.

CARTER, Raymond George – RHB RFM/OB

b. Small Heath, Birmingham, 14 April 1933. Educated at Billesley Secondary Modern School, Birmingham.

Debut 1951 v Scotland, Edgbaston 88 matches for W 1951–61; (professional – cap 1958). Highest score. W 37 v Cambridge U, Portland Road 1961. Best bowling: W 8–82 v Somerset, Edgbaston 1958 (14–136 in match).

Played one match for Combined Services 1952. Versatile bowler, pace or spin, forced into premature retirement due to back injury. Played for Sparkhill, and for Mitchells & Butlers in Birmingham League.

Groundsman at King's Heath CC; hockey for King's Heath.

Jack Bannister, Alan Townsend and Ray Carter (left to right) *seem to be saying, 'Who's got the biggest hands?'*

CARTWRIGHT, Thomas William – RHB RM

b. Coventry, 22 July 1935. Educated at Foxford School, Coventry.

Debut 1952 v Notts., Trent Bridge. 353 matches for W 1952–69 (professional – cap 1958). Benefit (£9,592) 1968. Highest score: W 210 v Middx., Griff & Coton, Nuneaton 1962 (adding 244 for 7th wicket with A.C. Smith). Best bowling: W 8–39 v Som., Weston-super-Mare 1962. Match analysis of 15–89 v Glam., Swansea 1967. 1000 runs (3); 1668 (30.89) 1961 best. 100 wickets (7); 147 (15.52) 1967 best. 'Double' 1962 – 1176 runs (33.60), 106 wickets (20.06).

Left Staffs. after 1969 season; Played 101 matches for Som. 1970–76; cap 1970; Testimonial 1975. Played 7 matches for Glam. 1977. Glam. Chief Coach since 1980. 5 Tests for England 1964–65: 6–94 in innings v S. Africa, Trent Bridge 1965. 15 Test wickets (36.26). 13710 runs (21.32); 1536 wickets (19.11) in first-class career.

Coached at Millfield School 1970–76.

CHARLESWORTH, Crowther – RHB RFM
b. Swinton, Lancs, 12 February 1875; d. Halifax, Yorks., 15 June 1953.

Debut v Surrey, The Oval 1898 (when not qualified). 372 matches for W 1898–1921 (professional – cap 1901). Benefit (£1,050) 1920. Highest score: W 216 v Derby., Blackwell Colliery 1910. Best bowling: W 6–45 v Derbys., Edgbaston 1901. 1000 runs (5); 1376 (38.22) 1911 best. When scoring 101* v Surrey, Edgbaston 1913 reached century in 70 minutes, still joint fastest for W.

Played for Moseley in Birmingham League.

CLARKSON, William
b. Lancashire.[1]

Debut 1922 v Cambridge U, Cambridge. 2 matches for W 1922–23. Highest score: W 41 v West Indies, Edgbaston 1923. Best bowling: W 2–24 same match.

Professional/groundsman for Lightcliffe (Bradford League) 1924–27.

---

[1] No further details of his birth or death are known.

CLAUGHTON, John Alan – RHB
b. Leeds, Yorks., 16 September 1956. Educated at King Edward's School, Edgbaston, Merton College, Oxford.

Debut 1979 v Lancs., Old Trafford. 18 matches for W 1979–80. Highest score: W 108* v Worcs., Worcester 1980.

Played for Oxford U 1976–79; Blue each year, Captain 1978. 51 and 112 on first-class debut, Oxford U v Gloucs., Oxford 1976. Gave up full-time cricket 1980 due to knee injury. Played for Berks. since 1982; present club Richmond.

Teacher at Eton. Great-uncle, H.M. Claughton, Yorks. professional 1914-19. Father, Ronald Claughton, Chairman W Supporters' Association.

bowling: W 2–75 v Middx., Edgbaston 1928.

For many years until 1986 public address announcer at Edgbaston. Played club cricket for King's Heath.

CLIFFORD, Christopher – RHB OB
b. Hovingham, Yorks., 5 July 1942. Educated at Malton Grammar School; Carnegie Hall College of Education, Leeds.

Debut v New Zealand, Edgbaston 1978. 36 matches for W 1978–80. Highest score: W 26 v Surrey, The Oval 1979. Best bowling: W 6–89 v Som., Weston-super-Mare 1978.

11 matches for Yorks. 1972. Club cricket for Scarborough.

Physical Education Teacher.

CLUGSTON, David Lindsey ('Lin') – LHB SLA
b. Belfast, N. Ireland, 5 February 1908.

Debut 1928 v Middx., Edgbaston. 3 matches 1928; 3 further matches 1946; an interval of 18 years between his 3rd and 4th matches for W. 6 matches for W 1928–46 (amateur). Highest score: W 17 v Notts., Coventry (Morris Motors) 1928. Best

COLLIN, Thomas – LHB SLA
b. South Moor, Stanley, Co. Durham, 7 April 1911.

Debut v Surrey, The Oval 1933. 52 matches for W 1933–36 (cap 1934). Highest score: W 105* v Glos., Edgbaston 1935. Best bowling: W 3–45 v Derby., Derby 1935. Added 199 with Tom Dollery v Gloucs., Edgbaston 1935 – County 7th wicket record until 1953.

Played for Durham County 1938–46; became Coach at Durham School.

COOK, David Roland – RHB LFM
b. Birmingham, 2 September 1936.
Educated at Warwick School.

Debut 1962 v Oxford U, Edgbaston. 9
matches for W 1962–68 (amateur). Highest
score: W 28* v Som., Taunton 1968. Best
bowling: W 4–66 v Yorks. Edgbaston 1967.

Played in Birmingham League for
Walsall (professional) and Moseley.

Rugby Union for Coventry and W.
Brother, M.S. Cook, played for W.

COOK, Michael Stephen – LHB WK
b. Birmingham, 19 February 1939.
Educated at Warwick School.

Debut 1961 v Cambridge U, Portland
Road. 2 matches for W 1961–62 (amateur).
Highest score: W 52 on debut.

Played for Aston Unity (Birmingham
League). Brother, D.R. Cook, played for
W.

COOKE, Robert – RHB RFM
b. Selly Oak, Birmingham, 25 May 1900;
d. Bournbrook, Birmingham, 14 January
1957.

Debut 1925 v Som., Edgbaston. 15
matches for W 1925–26 (professional).
Highest score: W 14 v Hants, Edgbaston
1925. Best bowling: W 5–22 v Kent,
Tunbridge Wells 1925 (took hat trick and 4
wickets in 5 balls).

Was Local Parks cricketer.

CORDNER, John Pruen – RHB LFM
b. Diamond Creek, Victoria, Australia, 20 March 1929. Educated at Melbourne Grammar School.

Debut 1952 v India, Edgbaston (only match – amateur). Played for W while on a course in Birmingham. Did not bat nor take any wickets.

3 matches for Victoria 1951–52. Played for West Bromwich Dartmouth (Birmingham League); U CC (Melbourne). Cousin L.O. Cordner played for Victoria.

Committee 1933–43; W Hon. Treasurer 1943–57.

Captain in Royal Navy.

COTTON, Robert Henry – RHB RFM
b. Birmingham, 5 November 1909; d. Warley, W. Midlands, 17 January 1979. Educated at Abbey Road School, Smethwick.

Debut 1947 v Lancs., Edgbaston. 2 matches for Warwickshire 1947 (amateur). Did not bat. Best bowling: W 2–42 v Sussex, Hove 1947.

Played in Birmingham League for Mitchells & Butlers and West Bromwich Dartmouth.

COWAN, Charles Frederic Roy – RHB
b. Glangrwyney, Brecon, 17 September 1883; d. Warwick, 22 March 1958.

Debut v Lancs., Liverpool 1909. 27 matches for W 1909–21 (amateur). Highest score: W 78 v Hants, Portsmouth 1920. W

CRANMER, Peter – RHB RMF
b. Acocks Green, Birmingham, 10 September 1914. Educated at St Edward's, Oxford and Christchurch College, Oxford.

Debut 1934 v Glos., Gloucester 1934. 166 matches for W 1934–54 (amateur – cap 1934 – Captain 1938–47). Highest score: W 113 v Northants, Edgbaston 1934. Best bowling: W 3–31 v Essex, Edgbaston 1946. 1000 runs (3); 1108 (21.72) 1947 best. W Committee 1948–85. Hon. Life Member, W CCC.

Played Indian Domestic Cricket 1944–45. Best bowling: 7–52; Services v Governor's XI, Calcutta 1944–45. 5853 Runs (21.60) in first-class career. Played for Cheshire in 1948. Club cricket for Moseley (Birmingham League) and Harborne.

Rugby Union for Oxford U, Moseley, Barbarians and England (16 caps, 2 as captain). Former sports commentator and journalist (cricket and Rugby Union football).

CRAWFORD, Alexander Basil – RHB RFM
b. Coleshill, W, 24 May 1891; d. in action, Ferme-du-Bois, near Richebourg, France, 10 May 1916. Educated at Oundle.

Debut 1911 v India, Edgbaston. 7 matches for W 1911 (amateur). Highest score: W 40 v Glos., Edgbaston 1911. Best bowling: W 6–36 v India on debut. 11 matches for Notts. 1912.

CRESSWELL, Joseph – RHB RMF
b. Denby, Derby., 22 December 1865; d. Birmingham, 19 July 1932.

Debut 1895 v Surrey, Edgbaston (non-first-class for W since 1889). 15 matches for W 1895–99 (Professional – cap before 1897). Highest score: W 16 v Essex, Edgbaston 1899. Best bowling: W 6–69 v Kent, Edgbaston 1896. Played for Mitchell's Brewery CC.

Later became groundsman at *Birmingham Post* and *Mail* Ground, Yardley, Birmingham. Nephew, J.A. Cresswell, played for Derby.

CRICHTON, Henry Thompson – RHB RM
b. Edgbaston, Birmingham, 18 May 1884; d. Poole, Dorset, 1 July 1968. Educated at King Edward's School, Birmingham.

Debut 1908 v Sussex, Edgbaston. 2 matches for W 1908 (amateur). Highest score: W 26 v Hants, Edgbaston 1908. Best bowling: W 2–21 v Sussex, Edgbaston 1908.

Played for Berks. 1913–14. Club cricket for Harborne.

CROCKFORD, Eric Bertram – RHB
b. Birmingham, 13 October 1888; d. Sutton Coldfield, 17 January 1958. Educated at Eastbourne.

Debut 1911 v India, Edgbaston. 21 matches for W 1911–22 (amateur –

Cheltenham 1930; 102 out of 204 v Lancs., Old Trafford 1931; 69 out of 133 v Leics., Hinckley 1936. Shared 18 century opening stands with Norman Kilner – W record.

Played for Berks. 1919–22; played for Moseley, Dudley in Birmingham League.

Son, L.C.B. Croom, played for W.

captained on occasions). Highest score: W 55 v Lancs., Old Trafford 1913. Best bowling: W 1–7 v Surrey, Edgbaston 1921.

Club cricket for Sutton Coldfield.

CROOM, Leslie Charles Bryan – RHB
b. Wynbunbury, Cheshire, 20 April 1920.

Debut 1949 v Cambridge U, Cambridge. 4 matches for W 1949 (professional). Highest score: W 26 v Essex, Brentwood 1949.

Played for West Bromwich Dartmouth (Birmingham League). Father, A.J.W. Croom, played for W.

CROOM, Alfred John William ('Arthur') – RHB RA Spin.
b. Reading, Berks., 23 May 1896; d. Oldbury, Worcs., 16 August 1947.

Debut 1922 v Cambridge U, Cambridge. 394 matches for W 1922–39; (professional – cap before 1926). Benefit (£679): 1936. Highest score: W 211 v Worcs., Edgbaston 1934. Best bowling: W 6–65 v Glam., Swansea 1930. 1000 runs (12); 1584 (39.60) 1931 best. Three centuries in consecutive innings 1931; 109 v Kent, Edgbaston; 105 v Northants, Peterborough; 159 v Notts., Edgbaston. Carried bat throughout innings 4 times – joint W record with Fred Gardner; 131 out of 311 v Northants, Edgbaston 1929; 58 out of 120 v Glos.,

CROSS, Anthony John – RHB
b. Fulmer, Bucks., 5 August 1945.
Educated at George Dixon's Grammar
School, Birmingham, and Fitzwilliam
College, Cambridge.

Debut 1969 v Scotland, Edgbaston (only
match). Highest score: W 20 in only match.

5 matches for Cambridge U 1966–67.

W Committee since 1983.

CROSS, Eric Percival – RHB WK
b. Handsworth Wood, Birmingham, 25
June 1896; d. Birmingham, 27 February
1985. Educated at Denstone.

Debut 1921 v Glos., Edgbaston. 7
matches for W 1921–23 (amateur). Highest
score: W 12* v Australia, Edgbaston 1921.

Played for Staffs. 1928–34; and for
Moseley (Birmingham League).

CUMBES, James – RHB RFM
b. East Didsbury, Manchester, 4 May
1944. Educated at Didsbury Technical
High School.

Debut 1982 v Cambridge U, Cambridge.
14 Matches for W 1982. Highest score: W
7* v Middlx., Coventry Courtaulds 1982.
Best bowling: W 4–64 v Oxford U, Oxford
1982.

First-class debut for Lancs. 1963; 9
matches 1963–67, 1971; 29 matches for
Surrey 1968–69; 109 matches for Worcs.
1972–81 (cap 1978). Highest first-class
score 43 Worcs. v Sussex, Hove 1980; best
bowling first-class 6–24 Worcs. v Yorks.,
Worcester 1977. 379 wickets (30.20) in

first-class career.

Joined W as player and Commercial
Manager 1982; retired from playing due to
illness. Played for West Bromwich
Dartmouth (Birmingham League).
Became Commercial Manager, Lancs.
CCC 1987.

Played soccer (goalkeeper) Tranmere
Rovers, West Bromwich Albion, Aston
Villa.

CURLE, Arthur Charles – LHB SLA
b. New Milverton, Leamington Spa, 27
July 1895; d. Aylesbury, Bucks., 2
February 1966. Educated at Leamington
College.

Debut 1920 v Cambridge U, Edgbaston.
3 matches for W 1920 (amateur). Highest
score: W 40 on debut.

1 match for Rhodesia 1922–23. Played
for Leamington CC and Raylton CC,
Bulawayo.

Brother, Gerald Curle, played for W.

CURLE, Gerald – RHB OB
b. New Milverton, Leamington Spa, 7 June
1893; d. Budleigh Salterton, Devon, 4
March 1977. Educated at King Edward's
School, Birmingham.

Debut 1913 v Hants, Edgbaston. 5
matches for W 1913. Highest score: W 34 v
Sussex, Coventry Butts 1913. Best
bowling: W 1–3 v Leics., Hinckley 1913.

Played for Leamington CC.

Brother, A.C. Curle, played for W and
Rhodesia.

DAVIES, Conrad Stephen – RHB SLA
b. Birmingham, 27 June 1907. Educated at
King Edward's Grammar School, Aston,
Birmingham.

Debut 1930 v Essex, Leyton. 8 matches
for W 1930–36 (amateur). Highest score:
W 63 v Kent, Tunbridge Wells 1933. Best
bowling: W 3–26 v Cambridge U,
Cambridge 1931. Played for Alexandra
Park CC (London) for 50 years from 1925.

President, Club Cricket Conference
1951.

DAVIES, Richard John – RHB RM
b. Selly Oak, Birmingham, 11 February
1954. Educated at Westlake High School,
Auckland, New Zealand, and Marple Hall
Grammar School.

Debut 1976 v Oxford U, Edgbaston
(only match). Highest score: W 18. Played
for Berks. 1979, Combined Services, the
Army.

DEMPSTER, Charles Stewart – RHB SRA
occasional WK
b. Wellington, New Zealand, 15
November 1903; d. Wellington, 14
February 1974. Educated at Wellington
Institute.

Debut 1946 v Sussex, Edgbaston 1946. 3
matches for W 1946 (amateur). Highest
score: W 40 v Sussex, Edgbaston. Left W
after objections from Leics. regarding
qualification, and returned to New
Zealand.

Played Wellington (New Zealand)
1921–22 to 1947–48. 1 match Scotland
1934; 65 matches Leics. 1935–39 (cap 1936;
captain 1936–38). 10 Tests for New
Zealand 1929–30 to 1932–33; 723 runs
(65.72). Highest score in Tests 136 v
England, Wellington 1929–30. Highest
first-class score 212, New Zealanders v
Essex, Leyton 1931. 12145 runs (44.98)
and 35 centuries in first-class cricket.
Played for Smethwick in Birmingham
League.

DEVEY, John Henry George – RHB RM
b. Newtown, Birmingham, 26 December 1866; d. Moseley, Birmingham, 11 October 1940. Educated at Farm Street Board School, Hockley, Birmingham.

Debut 1894 v Yorks. Edgbaston (non-first-class from 1888). 153 matches for W 1894–1907 (professional – cap by 1897). Benefit (£400) 1906. Highest score: W 246 v Derby., Edgbaston 1900 (then W record). Best bowling: W 3–65 v Surrey, The Oval 1895. 1237 runs (41.23) 1906.

Played for Aston Unity and Mitchells CC (Birmingham League).

Brilliant soccer player, Aston Villa and England; captain and, later, director, Aston Villa.

(played non-first-class 1893). 118 matches for W 1894–1901 (professional – cap by 1895). Highest score: W 184 v Leics., Edgbaston 1899. Best bowling: W 6–58 v Notts., Trent Bridge 1894 (on debut). (These were his only wickets in first-class cricket.) 1010 runs (31.56) 1899. First professional to captain W, v Essex, Leyton 1899.

Played for Surrey 1883–86; amateur 1883–85; professional 1886. Represented both Gentlemen and Players in first-class matches. Played for Moseley in Birmingham League; later played for Newport and Monmouth CCC.

Soccer for Aston Villa (goalkeeper).

DICKENS, Frederick – LHB LM
b. Stratford-upon-Avon, 23 April 1873; d. Warwick, 20 February 1935. Educated at Stratford-upon-Avon Board School.

Debut 1898 v Derby., Derby. 29 matches for W 1898–1903 (professional – capped by 1900). Highest score: W 35 v Leics., Leicester 1898. Best bowling: W 6–23 v Derby., Derby 1899 (11–45 match).

Played for Handsworth Wood (Birmingham League) and Stratford-upon-Avon. Later groundsman, Leamington.

DIVER, Edwin James ('Teddy') – RHB RM Lobs occ. WK
b. Cambridge, 20 March 1861; d. Pontardawe, South Wales, 27 December 1924. Educated at Perse School, Cambridge.

Debut 1894 v Notts., Trent Bridge

DOBSON, Frederick – RHB SLA
b. Olton, Solihull, 12 October 1898; d. Burley, Hants, 15 October 1980. Educated at Tettenhall College.

Debut 1928 v Glam., Edgbaston. 3 matches for W 1928 (amateur). Highest score: W 7, on debut. Best bowling: W 3–51 v Som., Edgbaston 1928.

Played for Olton CC.

DOBSON, Kenneth William Cecil – RHB
b. Shardlow, Derby., 28 August 1900; d. Newton Abbott, Devon, 3 March 1960. Educated at Repton.

Debut 1925 v Northants, Kettering. 2 matches for W 1925 (amateur). Highest score: W 12* v Hants, Southampton 1925.

3 matches for Derby. 1920; also played Staffs.

Uncles, W.S. and J.T.C. Eadie, played for Derby.

DOCKER, Ludford Charles – RHB

b. Smethwick, Staffs., 26 November 1860; d. Stratford-upon Avon, 1 August 1940. Educated at King Edward's School, Birmingham.

Debut 1894 v Kent, Edgbaston (played non-first-class from 1887). 11 matches for W 1894–95 (amateur). Highest score: W 85* v Yorks., Edgbaston 1894.

Played for Derby. (first-class) 1881–85 – captain 1884. Left Derby. on discovery of birthplace. Toured Australia with a Shrewsbury's XI 1887–88. 2665 runs (20.82) in first-class cricket. Played for Handsworth Wood in Birmingham League. Presented the Docker Shield for competition between Birmingham Schools, 1886.

Brothers F.D. and M.R. Docker played for Derby.

DOLLERY, Horace Edgar ('Tom') – RHB; occ WK

b. Reading, Berks., 14 October 1914; d. Queen Elizabeth Hospital, Birmingham, 22 January 1987. Educated at Reading School.

Debut 1934 v Yorks., Scarborough. 413 matches for W 1934–55 (professional – cap 1935). Joint-captain with R.H. Maudsley 1948; sole captain 1949–55. Benefit (£6,362) 1949. Highest score: W 212 v Leics., Edgbaston 1952. 1000 runs (15); 2084 (47.36) 1949 best. Added 220 for 6th wicket with Jack Buckingham v Derby., Derby 1938 and 250 for 7th wicket with Jimmie Ord v Kent, Maidstone 1953 – both W records. W coach 1956–59; W Committee 1964–72.

Played for Wellington (Plunkett Shield) 1950–51. 4 Tests for England 1947–50; 72 runs (10.28). 24413 runs (37.50), 52 centuries, in first-class career. Test selector 1957–58. Played for Berks. 1931–33. Played for Smethwick in Birmingham League.

Soccer for Reading.

Warwickshire take the field at Clacton on 23 August 1951. Note the rare sight of Tom Dollery (centre) *wearing a cap*

DOLLERY, Keith Robert – RHB RFM
b. Cooroy, Queensland, Australia, 9 December 1924.
    Debut 1951 v S. Africa, Edgbaston. 73 matches for W 1951–56 (professional – cap 1954). Highest score: W 41 v Som., Edgbaston 1954. Best bowling: W 8–42 v Sussex, Edgbaston 1954. Hat tricks v Glos., Bristol 1953, and v Kent, Coventry Courtaulds 1956.
    First-class debut for Queensland 1947–48; played for Auckland (New Zealand) 1949–50 and for Tasmania 1950–51. League cricket Mitchells & Butlers (Birmingham League) and Stockport.

DONALD, Allan Anthony – RHB RF
b. Bloemfontein, S. Africa, 20 October 1966. Educated at Grey College Bloemfontein; Technical High School, Bloemfontein.
    Debut 1987 v Glam., Edgbaston. 18

matches for W 1987–88. Highest score: W 37 v Sussex, Griff & Coton, Nuneaton 1987. Best bowling: W 5–42 v Leics., Edgbaston 1987.

First-class debut Orange Free State 1985–86. Best bowling: first-class cricket 8–37, Orange Free State v Transvaal at Jo'burg 1986–87.

DONNELLY, Martin Paterson – LHB occ SLA
b. Ngaruawahia, New Zealand, 17 October 1917. Educated at New Plymouth High School, Canterbury U and Worcester College, Oxford.

Debut 1948 v Derby., Derby 1948. 20 matches for W 1948–50 (amateur – cap 1948 – captain on occasions). Highest score: W 120 v Yorks., Edgbaston 1948. W Committee 1948–50.

First-class debut for Wellington 1936–37; 5 matches for Wellington 1936–37 to 1937–38; 1940–41; 6 matches for Canterbury 1938–39 to 1939–40; 23 matches for Oxford U 1946–47; Blue both years, captain 1947; 1 match for Middlx. 1946. 7 Tests for New Zealand 1937–49: 582 runs (52.90); highest score 206 v England, Lord's 1949. Highest first-class score 208* MCC v Yorks., Scarborough 1948. Scored 2287 runs, average 61.81 for New Zealand Tourists in England 1949. 9250 runs (47.43) in first-class career. Played for Taranaki (New Zealand), Smethwick (Birmingham League), Castleton Moor.

Rugby Union for Oxford, Blackheath, England (1 cap).

DOSHI, Dilip Rasiklal – LHB SLA
b. Rajkot, India, 22 December 1947. Educated at J.J. Ajmera High School, Calcutta; St Xavier's College, Calcutta U.

Debut 1980 v Oxford U, Oxford. 43

matches for W 1980–81 (cap 1980). Highest score: W 35 v Middx., Lord's 1981. Best bowling: W 6–72 v Som., Taunton 1980 101 wickets (26.73) in 1980 (debut season).

Played for Bengal 1968–69 to 1985–86; Saurashtra 1986–87; 44 matches for Notts. 1973–78 (cap 1977); 33 Tests for India 1979–80 to 1983–84; 114 wickets (30.72). Best bowling 6–103 v Australia, Madras 1979–80; 898 wickets (26.58) in first-class cricket. Played for Herts. 1976, Northumb. 1979. Birmingham League for Walsall.

DUNKELS, Paul Renton – LHB RM
b. Marylebone, London, 26 November 1947. Educated at Harrow.

Debut 1971 v India, Edgbaston (only match).

1 first-class match for Minor Counties 1971; 1 first-class match for Sussex 1972. Highest first-class score 3* Sussex v Cambridge U, Cambridge 1972. Best first-class bowling 2–60 same match. Played for Devon 1969–75 and club cricket for Torquay.

6ft 9 in tall – tallest ever W cricketer.

DURNELL, Thomas Wilfred – RHB RF
b. Cannon Hill, Birmingham, 17 June 1901; d. Hexham, Northumb., 10 April 1986. Educated at Tindall Street School.

Debut 1921 v Yorks., Sheffield. 14 matches for W 1921–30 (amateur). Highest

score: W 5* on debut. Best bowling: W 7–29 (10–89 match) v Northants, Edgbaston 1927.

Played for Smethwick (Birmingham League) 28 years.

DYER, Robin Ian Henry Benbow ('Dobbin') – RHB
b. Hertford, 22 December 1958. Educated at Wellington College and Durham U.

Debut 1981 v Leics., Coventry Courtaulds. 65 matches for W 1981–86. Highest score: W 109* v Zimbabweans, Edgbaston 1985. 1000 runs (2); 1187 (34.91) 1984 best.

Debut 1947 v Essex, Coventry Courtaulds (only match – amateur). Highest score 4.

Played Coventry and North W 1931–66. Squash for W. Son 'Pip' Elson, well-known professional golfer.

EDMONDS, Roger Bertram – RHB RM/OB
b. Birmingham, 2 March 1941. Educated at Saltley Grammar School and Loughborough Colleges.

Debut 1962 v Middx., Lord's 1962. 78 matches for W 1962–67 (professional). Highest score: W 102* v Scotland, Edgbaston 1966. Best bowling: W 5–40 v Derby., Derby 1963.

Played for Aston Unity and Moseley in Birmingham League.

ELSON, Geoffrey ('Gus') – LHB SLA
b. Coventry, 19 March 1913. Educated at Rydal School.

EVERITT, Russell Stanley – RHB
b. King's Heath, Birmingham, 8 September 1881; d. Kew Gardens, Surrey, 11 May 1973. Educated at Malvern College.

Debut 1909 v Surrey, The Oval. 3 matches for W 1909. (Amateur) captain on debut. Highest score: W 38 on debut.

1 match for Worcs. 1901. Played for Moseley (Birmingham League), Olton, Richmond (Surrey).

FABLING, Arthur Hugh – RHB occ WK
b. Grandborough, 6 September 1888; d. Grandborough, 11 October 1972. Educated at Wellingborough.

Debut v Northants, Northampton 1921 (only match – amateur). Highest score: W 7.

Played for Rugby CC. Soccer for Northampton Town.

FARREN, George Clement – RHB
b. Rugby *c* 1873;[1] d. Coventry, 2 November 1956.

Debut 1912 v Yorks. Hull (only match – amateur). Scored 0 in only innings.

Played for Coventry and North W.

[1] It has been impossible to obtain full date of birth.

FANTHAM, William Edward – RHB OB
b. Birmingham, 14 May 1918.

Debut 1935 v Glos., Gloucester. 63 matches for W 1935–48 (professional – cap 1946). Highest score: W 51 v Notts., Edgbaston 1946. Best bowling: W 5–55 v Somerset, Edgbaston 1946.

Played for Mitchells & Butlers in Birmingham League; also professional in Coventry League.

FERREIRA, Anthonie Michal ('Anton', 'Yogie') – RHB RM
b. Pretoria, S. Africa, 13 April 1955. Educated at Hill View High School, Pretoria; Pretoria U.

Debut 1979 v Middx., Lord's. 138 matches for W 1979–86 (cap 1983). Highest score: W 112* v India, Edgbaston 1982. Best bowling: W 6–70 v Leics., Edgbaston 1984.

Highest first-class score 133 Northern Transvaal v Natal, Durban 1986–87. Best first-class bowling 8–38 Northern Transvaal v Transvaal 'B', Pretoria 1977–78. Has played for Northern Transvaal since 1974–75. 7860 runs (28.17); 5 centuries; 564 wickets (30.30) in first-class career. Two one-day internationals, S. Africa v Australia, 1985–86.

Highest score: W 39 v Glos., Cheltenham 1908. Best bowling: W 9–104 (13–192 match) v Leics., Leicester 1899. 100 wickets (2); 128 (20.52) 1911 best. Hat trick (and 5 wickets in 7 balls) v Hants, Edgbaston 1911.

1026 wkts (23.48) in all first-class cricket. First-class umpire 1927–34.

FIDDIAN-GREEN, Charles Anderson Fiddian – RHB occ RM
b. Handsworth, Birmingham, 22 December 1898; d. Malvern, Worcs., 5 September 1976. Educated at The Leys School, Jesus College, Cambridge.

Debut v Cambridge U, Edgbaston 1920. 64 matches for W 1920–28 (amateur). Highest score: W 95 v Sussex, Coventry Butts 1924.

Cambridge Blue 1921–22; played for Worcs. 24 matches 1931–34. 4350 runs (31.07) in all first-class cricket.

Hockey, Cambridge U and England.

FIELD, Ernest Frank – RHB RF
b. Weethley Hamlet, W, 23 September 1874; d. Droitwich, Worcs., 25 August 1934.

Debut 1897 v Lancs., Edgbaston. 256 matches for W 1897–1920 (professional – capped c 1900). Benefit (£620) 1912.

FIELD, Maxwell Nicholas – RHB RM
b. Coventry, 23 March 1950. Educated at

Bablake School, Coventry, London U and Emmanuel College, Cambridge.

Debut 1974 v Pakistan, Edgbaston. 3 matches for W 1974–75. Highest score: W 1* on debut. No wickets.

Cambridge Blue 1974. Highest first-class score 39* Cambridge U v W, Cambridge 1974. Best first-class bowling 4–76 in 1974 U match. Played West Bromwich Dartmouth (Birmingham League).

FLAHERTY, Kevin Frederick – RHB OB
b. Birmingham, 17 September 1939. Educated at George Dixon's Grammar School, Birmingham.

Debut 1969 v Cambridge U, Edgbaston (only match). Best bowling: W 3–38.

Now coaching in Australia.

FISHWICK, Tom Silvester – RHB
b. Stone, Staffs., 24 July 1876; d. Sandown, Isle of Wight, 21 February 1950. Educated at Wellingborough.

Debut 1896 v Derby., Edgbaston. 206 matches for W 1896–1909 (amateur – capped c 1900; joint-captain 1902 with H.W. Bainbridge; 1907 with J.F. Byrne). Highest score: W 140* v Derby., Edgbaston 1901. 1000 runs (2); 1353 (33.00) 1905 best. Centuries before lunch on two occasions: 131 v Glos., Bristol 1900; 113 v Leics., Leicester 1904 (both on first morning of match). 5 catches in match, v S. Africa, Edgbaston 1904; record until 1962. 40 catches in season 1905; record until 1951.

Played for Handsworth Wood (Birmingham League).

FLETCHER, Barry Elystan – LHB occ WK
b. Birmingham, 7 March 1935. Educated at

Bishop Vesey's Grammar School, Sutton Coldfield, and Colwyn Bay Grammar School.

Debut 1956 v Combined Services, Edgbaston. 49 matches for W 1956–61 (professional). Highest score: W 102* v Oxford U, Edgbaston 1960.

Played for Moseley and Mitchells & Butlers in Birmingham League; also Colwyn Bay.

Played badminton for Wales.

1951. Father, Ben Flint (Notts); uncle, W.A. Flint (Notts); wife, Rachel Heyhoe-Flint former England Women's captain.

FLICK, Barry John – RHB WK
b. Coventry, 5 March 1952. Educated at Caludon Castle School, Coventry.

Debut 1969 v Cambridge U, Edgbaston 1969. 16 matches for W 1969–73. Highest score: W 18 v Glos., Cheltenham 1973.

Played for Aston Unity (Birmingham League), for Coventry and for North W.

FLINT, Derrick – RHB LBG
b. Creswell, Derby., 14 June 1924.

Debut 1948 v Cambridge U, Edgbaston. 10 matches for W 1948–49 (professional). Highest score: W 11 v Derby., Edgbaston 1948. Best bowling: W 4–67 v Cambridge U, Edgbaston 1948.

Played for Coventry and North W, Harborne and Walsall (Birmingham League).

Professional coach, Dean Close School

FLOWER, Russell William – LHB SLA
b. Stone, Staffs., 6 November 1942. Educated at Granville School, Stone.

Debut 1978 v Surrey, Edgbaston. 9 matches for W 1978. Highest score: W 10* v Yorks., Bradford 1978. Best bowling: W 3–45 v Northants, Northampton 1978.

Played for Staffordshire 1964–77; 1979–date. Plays for Stone CC.

FORRESTER, Thomas – LHB RMF

b. Clay Cross, Derby., 21 September 1873; d. Nottingham, 27 December 1927. Educated at Tilton Road Board School, Small Heath, Birmingham; Saltley College, Birmingham.

Debut 1896 v Leics., Leicester 1896. 26 matches for W 1896–99 (amateur). Highest score: W 38 v Yorks., Edgbaston 1897. Best bowling: W 7–56 v Hants, Edgbaston 1896.

105 matches for Derby. 1902–20. 347 wickets (25.70) in all first-class matches. Played Dudley in Birmingham League.

FOSTER, Arthur Webster – RHB WK

b. Deritend, Birmingham, 12 August 1894; d. Hall Green, Birmingham, 9 January 1954. Educated at Repton.

Debut 1914 v Northants, Edgbaston (only match – amateur). Highest score: W 1*.

Brother, F.R. Foster (W and England).

FOSTER, Derek George – RHB RF

b. Sutton Coldfield, 19 March 1907; d. Chipping Campden, Glos., 13 October 1980. Educated at Shrewsbury School.

Debut 1928 v Surrey, Edgbaston. 52 matches for W 1928–34 (amateur). Highest score: W 70 (including 5 sixes) v Som., Taunton 1931. Best bowling: W 7–42 v Surrey, The Oval 1930.

Played for Mitchells & Butlers and Moseley in Birmingham League; also Sutton Coldfield.

Once threw cricket ball 133 yards while at school; in 1930 created Danish record (about 130 yards).

FOSTER, Frank Rowbotham – RHB LFM

b. Deritend, Birmingham, 31 January 1889; d. Northampton, 3 May 1958. Educated at Solihull Grammar School.

Debut 1908 v Derby., Derby. 127 matches for W 1908–14 (amateur – cap 1908 – captain 1911–14). Highest score: W 305* v Worcs., Dudley 1914 (W record score). Best bowling: W 9–118 v Yorks., Edgbaston 1911.

'Doubles':

> 1911 1459 runs (42.91) and 124 wickets (19.69);
> 1914 1396 runs (34.90) and 117 wickets (18.25)
> 11 Tests for England 1911–12 to 1912;

330 runs (23.57); 45 wickets (20.57). 6548 runs (26.61) 718 wickets (20.72) in first-class career. Played for Moseley (Birmingham League) and Hall Green.

Career ended by road accident during 1914–18 war. Brother, A.W. Foster (W).

FOX, John George – RHB WK
b. Norton-on-Tees, Co. Durham, 22 July 1929.

Debut 1959 v Northants, Northampton. 43 matches for W 1959–61 (professional).

Highest score: W 52 v India, Edgbaston 1959.

Played for Co. Durham 1950–58; 62–64; Devon 1968–69.

FOX, John – LHB SLA
b. Selly Park, Birmingham, 7 September 1904; d. Birmingham, 15 November 1961.

Debut 1922 v Worcs., Stourbridge. 46 matches for W 1922–28 (professional). Highest score: W 27* v Leics., Leicester 1927. Best bowling: W 4–27 v Worcs., Edgbaston 1926.

94 matches for Worcs. 1929–33; 2907 runs (16.70) and 46 wickets (47.67) in first-class career.

FRANKLIN, Reginald Carey – RHB
b. Radford Fields, Coventry, 30 April 1880; d. Saltdean, Brighton, 25 June 1957. Educated at Repton.

Debut 1900 v Derby., Glossop (only match – amateur).

Played for Kenilworth CC.

GARDNER, Fred Charles – RHB
b. Bell Green, Coventry, 4 June 1922; d. Coventry, 13 January 1979. Educated at Windmill Road School, Coventry.

Debut 1947 v Glos., Edgbaston. 338 matches for W 1947-61; (amateur 1947, then professional – cap 1949). Benefit (£3,750) 1958. Highest score: W 215* v Som., Taunton 1950. 1000 runs (10); 1911 (45.50) 1950 best. 113 and 101* in match, v Essex, Ilford 1950. Carried bat throughout innings 4 times – joint W record with Arthur Croom; 140 out of 283 v Worcs., Edgbaston 1949; 73 out of 133 v Glam., Swansea 1950; 184 out of 286 v Lancs., Liverpool 1952; 62 out of 149 v Glam., Edgbaston 1954.

Played League cricket in Coventry.

First-class umpire 1962-65. Soccer for Newport County, Birmingham, Northampton Town, Coventry City.

GARDOM, Barry Keith – RHB LB
b. Birmingham, 31 December 1952. Educated at Bishop Vesey's Grammar School, Sutton Coldfield.

Debut 1973 v Cambridge U, Edgbaston. 18 matches for W 1973-74. Highest score: W 79* v Surrey, Edgbaston 1974. Best bowling: W 6-139 v Essex, Chelmsford 1974.

GAUNT, Howard Charles Adie – RHB
b. Edgbaston, Birmingham, 13 November 1902; d. Winchester, Hants, 1 February 1983. Educated at Tonbridge and King's College, Cambridge.

Debut 1919 v Worcs., Worcester (aged 16 with two years remaining at school). 11 matches for W 1919-22 (amateur). Highest score: W 32 v Som., Edgbaston 1922.

Hockey and lawn tennis for W. Church of England priest; became Precentor of Winchester Cathedral.

GEORGE, William – RHB
b. Shrewsbury, Salop., 29 June 1874; d.

N.F. Horner (left) *and F.C. Gardner about to embark on their
record-breaking innings against Australia in 1953*

Selly Oak, Birmingham, 4 December 1933.

Debut 1901 v S. Africa, Edgbaston. 13 matches for W 1901–06 (professional). Highest score: W 71 v Hants, Basingstoke 1906.

Played for Aston Unity (Birmingham League), Yardley, Kings Heath. Played as goalkeeper for Aston Villa and England.

Debut 1983 v Lancs., Edgbaston. 139 matches for W 1983–88 (cap 1983 – captain 1985–87). Highest score: W 39 v Leics., Edgbaston 1983. Best bowling: W 6–22 v Middx., Edgbaston 1983. 104 wickets (23.01) 1983.

521 matches for Worcs. 1960–82 (cap 1961 – captain 1971–80); Benefit (£11,047) 1974, Testimonial 1981. 100 wickets in all first-class matches 4 times. Highest first-class score 89 Worcs. v Oxford U, Oxford 1963. Best first-class bowling 8–28 Worcs. v Yorks., Sheffield 1968. 15 Tests for England 1964–73; 33 wickets (31.09). 2068 wickets (23.56) in first-class cricket. Played for Dudley in Birmingham League.

Test selector 1982. Awarded MBE 1982.

GIBBS, Lancelot Richard ('Lance') – RHB OB

b. Georgetown, British Guiana (now Guyana), 29 September 1934. Educated at Standard High School, Georgetown.

Debut 1967 v Cambridge U, Edgbaston 1967. 109 matches for W 1967–72 (cap 1968). Highest score: W 24 v Glam., Edgbaston 1972. Best bowling: W 8–37 v Glam., Edgbaston 1970. 131 wickets (18.89) 1971.

Played for British Guiana (Guyana) 1953–54 to 1974–75; S. Australia 1969–70. 79 Tests for W. Indies 1957–58 to 1975–76; 309 wickets (29.09); best bowling 8–38 v India, Bridgetown 1961–62. 1024 wickets (27.22) in first-class career.

Now in Sports Administration. Cousin, Clive Lloyd (W. Indies).

GIFFORD, Norman – LHB SLA

b. Ulverston, Lancs., 30 March 1940. Educated at Ulverston Secondary School.

GITTINS, Albert Edward – RHB RM

b. Southport, Lancs., 12 September 1897; d. Ladywood, Birmingham, 6 October 1977.

Debut 1919 v Glos., Cheltenham. 2 matches for W 1919 (professional). Highest score: W 2 v Worcs., Worcester 1919. Best bowling: W 2–17 same match.

Played for West Birmingham CC.

Played for Staffs. 1893–94; and for Handsworth Wood (Birmingham League).

GLASSFORD, John – RHB RFM
b. Sunderland, Co. Durham 20 July 1946.
Educated at Haswell Secondary School.

Debut 1969 v Cambridge U, Edgbaston.
2 matches for W 1969. No runs. Best
bowling: W 2–9 on debut.

Played for Durham County 1968–74:
professional with several clubs in Durham.

GLOVER, Alfred Charles Stirrup – RHB
RM
b. Stoke-on-Trent, Staffs., 19 April 1872;
d. Kenilworth, 22 May 1949. Educated at
Repton.

Debut 1895 v Essex, Edgbaston. 149
matches for W 1895–1909 (captain
1908–09). Highest score: W 124 v Yorks.,
Edgbaston 1904. Best bowling: W 5–21 v
Kent, Canterbury 1895. 1011 runs (40.44)
in 1904. Scored 199* before lunch, Day 3
of match v Hants, Edgbaston 1899 204
added with W.G. Quaife v Worcs.,
Worcester 1908 (6th wicket record for W
until 1938).

GLYNN, Brian Thomas – RHB OB
b. Birmingham, 27 April 1940.

Debut 1959 v Scotland, Edgbaston. 2
matches for W 1959–61 (professional).

Highest score: W 7 v Scotland, Edgbaston 1961.

Played for West Bromwich Dartmouth (Birmingham League).

GOBEY, Stanley Clarke ('Mick') – LHB RM
b. Stafford, 18 June 1916.

Debut 1946 v Derby., Derby 1946. 2 matches for W 1946 (amateur). Highest score: W 2 on debut.

Played for Bournville.

GOODWAY, Cyril Clement – RHB WK
b. Smethwick, Staffs., 10 July 1909.

Educated at Bourne College, Quinton.

Debut 1937 v Worcs., Edgbaston 1937. 40 matches for W 1937–47 (amateur – cap 1939). Highest score: W 37* v Glam., Edgbaston 1946. On W Committee 1945–72; Chairman, W Committee 1972–83. Now W Life Member.

Played for Staffs. 1933–36 and for Smethwick in Birmingham League.

GOODWIN, Harold James – RHB LB
b. Edgbaston, Birmingham, 31 January 1886; d. in action, Arras, France, 24 April 1917. Educated at Marlborough and Jesus College, Cambridge.

Debut 1912 v Northants, Peterborough 1912. 19 matches for W 1907–12 (amateur – captain 1910). Highest score: W 101 v Sussex, Hove 1908. Best bowling: W 4–35 v Worcs., Worcester 1910. W Committee 1914–17.

Played for Cambridge 1906–08 (Blue 1907–08). 1255 Runs (19.92) and 86 wickets (24.32) in first-class career.

Played hockey for Cambridge U and England.

GORDON, Alan – RHB
b. Coventry, 29 March 1944. Educated at King Henry VII School, Coventry.

Debut 1966 v Oxford U, Edgbaston. 34

1920. 1000 runs (2); 1404 (34.24) 1925 best. 98 wickets (23.85) 1920.

First-class debut for Sussex 1911; 2 matches 1911–12. Cambridge U 1913–14; 1919. Blue each year. 4 Tests for England (v W. Indies) 1929–30 (captain); 129 runs (18.42); 1 wicket for 91 runs. 12596 runs (24.03); 782 wickets (29.91) in first-class career. Achieved 'Double' in all first-class matches 1920 (1025 runs – 22.77; 100 wickets – 24.26). Played for Handsworth Wood in Birmingham League.

Member of Calthorpe family, owners of Calthorpe Estate on which Edgbaston stands.

GRANVILLE, Richard St Leger – RHB
b. Kingsworthy, Hants, 24 April 1907; d. Hitchin, Herts., 8 August 1972. Educated at Eton.

Debut 1934 v Leics., Edgbaston (only match – amateur). Highest score: W 7.

matches for W 1966–71. Highest score: W 65 v Surrey, The Oval 1970.

Played for Coventry and North W.

GRAY, John Denis – LHB LMF
b. Meriden, 9 October 1948. Educated at Woodlands School, Coventry and Loughborough College.

Debut 1968 v Scotland, Edgbaston. 7 matches for W 1968–69. Highest score: W 18 v Surrey, Edgbaston 1969. Best bowling: W 5–2 v Scotland on debut.

Played for Morris Motors, North Sydney. Played rugby football for Coventry and Warwickshire; top-class Rugby League for Wigan, Rest of World and Great Britain.

GOUGH-CALTHORPE, Frederick **Somerset** – RHB RMF
b. Kensington, London, 27 May 1892; d. Worplesdon, Surrey, 19 November 1935. Educated at Repton and Jesus College, Cambridge.

Debut 1919 v Derby., Derby. 231 matches for W 1919–30 (amateur – cap 1919 – captain 1920–29). Highest score: W 209 v Hants, Edgbaston 1921. Best bowling: W 5–20 v Yorks., Harrogate

GRAYLAND, Albert Victor – RHB RFM
b. Small Heath, Birmingham, 24 March 1900; d. Birmingham, 3 February 1963.

Debut 1922 v Som., Taunton. 4 matches for W 1922–30 (professional). Highest

score: W 6* v Som., Edgbaston 1922. Best bowling: W 1–23 on debut.

Played Parks cricket, Small Heath; subsequently professional in Coventry League.

GREEN, John Herbert – RHB SLA
b. Kenilworth, 9 May 1908; d. Broadstairs, Kent, 13 September 1987. Educated at Brighton College and Brasenose, Oxford.

Debut 1927 v Worcs., Worcester (only match – amateur). 0* in only innings.

Became Headmaster, Selwyn School, Broadstairs.

GREEN, Simon James – RHB
b. Bloxwich, Staffs., 19 March 1970. Educated at Old Swinford Hospital, Worcester.

Debut 1988 v Lancs., Nuneaton – Griff & Coton (only match). Highest score: W 28 – after being dismissed 1st ball 1st innings.

Played for Moseley in Birmingham League.

GREENING, Thomas – RHB OB
b. in Scotland, 1883; d. Leamington Spa, 25 March 1956.

Debut 1912 v Derby., Derby. 2 matches for W 1912 (amateur). Highest score: W 14 v Yorks. Edgbaston 1912. Best bowling: W 1–35 on debut.

Played for Handsworth Wood (Birmingham League) and Coventry and North W.

GRIFFITHS, Shirley – RHB RF
b. Barbados, 11 July 1930. Educated at St

Mark's College, Bridgetown, Barbados.

Debut 1956 v Cambridge U, Cambridge. 27 matches for W 1956–58 (professional). Highest score: W 17* v Surrey, Edgbaston 1957. Best bowling: W 7–62 v Kent, Edgbaston 1958.

Played for Moseley (Birmingham League), Middlesbrough, Lancaster.

100 wickets (2); 118 (17.13) 1952 Best. Scorer for W 1974–81.

15 matches for Worcs. 1954. 744 wickets (22.66) in first-class career. Played for Mitchells & Butlers, Old Hill, Smethwick at various times in Birmingham League.

GROSS, Frederick Albert – RHB LBG
b. Southampton, Hants, 17 September 1902; d. Birmingham, 11 March 1975. Educated at King Edward's Grammar School, Southampton.

Debut 1934 v Yorks., Edgbaston 1934 (only match – professional). 0* and 1–76 in only match.

34 matches for Hants 1924–29 as amateur. Came to Birmingham 1930 for engineering employment and played for Mitchells & Butlers (Birmingham League) as professional. 51 wickets (37.76) in first-class career.

GROVE, Charles William – RHB RMF
b. Birmingham, 16 December 1912; d. Solihull 15 February 1982. Educated at Yardley Secondary School.

Debut 1938 v Northants, Edgbaston 201 matches for W 1938–53 (professional – cap 1947). Benefit (£4,464) 1951. Highest score: W 104* v Leics., Leicester 1948. Best bowling: W 9–39 (8 wickets before lunch) v Sussex, Edgbaston 1952. Also took 8–38 v W. Indians, Edgbaston 1950.

GUY, John Bernard – RHB LM
b. Ramsgate, Kent, 16 May 1916. Educated at Chatham House, Ramsgate; Brasenose College, Oxford.

Debut 1950 v Glos., Edgbaston. 2 matches for W 1950 (amateur). Highest score: W 18 v Glos., Edgbaston 1950.

6 matches for Oxford U 1938–39; 1 match for Kent 1939. Played for St George's CC, Ramsgate, St Lawrence CC, Canterbury, Harborne.

H

HACKING, John Kenneth – RHB RM
b. Kenilworth, 21 March 1909. Educated at
Warwick School.
Debut 1946 v Lancs., Old Trafford (only
match – amateur). Highest score: W 14.
Played for Moseley Ashfield CC.

HALL, William ('Sol') – RHB RF
b. Bedworth, 7 April 1878; d. Bedworth
area *c* 1930.[1]

Debut 1905 v Oxford U, Oxford. 2
matches for W 1905 (professional).
Highest score: W 8 v Australia, Edgbaston
1905.
Played for Bedworth Cricket Club.

[1] Despite numerous enquiries it has not been
possible to discover the exact date of death of
'Sol' Hall; he left no close relatives and the
several, more distant relatives traced can offer
no exact information.

HAMPTON, William Marcus – RHB SRA
b. Bromsgrove, Worcs., 20 January 1903;
d. Ringwood, Hants, 7 April 1964.
Educated at Clifton College and
Emmanuel College, Cambridge.
Debut 1922 v Northants, Edgbaston
1922 (only match – amateur). Highest
score: W 34.
12 matches for Worcs. 1925–26.
Became Assistant Master, Winchester.

HANDS, Barry Onslow – LHB ROB
b. Moseley, Birmingham, 26 September 1916; d. Birmingham, 1 July 1984. Educated at Woodrough School, Birmingham.

Debut 1946 v Leics., Barwell. 3 matches for W 1946–47 (amateur). Highest score: W 9 on debut. Best bowling: W 3–76 v Glam., Swansea 1947.

Played for Moseley (Birmingham League) and Moseley Ashfield.

Uncle, W.C. Hands, played for W.

HANDS, William Cecil – RHB RFM
b. Sparkhill, Birmingham, 20 December

1886; d. Northwood, Middlesex, 31 August 1974. Educated at King Edward's Grammar School, Camp Hill, Birmingham.

Debut 1909 v Surrey, The Oval. 60 matches for W 1909–20 (amateur – capped). Highest score: W 63 v Lancs., Old Trafford 1919. Best bowling: W 5–10 v Surrey, The Oval 1912.

Played for Camp Hill Old Edwardian CC.

HARRIS, Archibald John – RHB
b. Rugby, 22 December 1892; d. Lymington, Hants, 10 April 1955. Educated at Rugby School.

Debut 1919 v Worcs., Worcester (only match – amateur). Highest score: W 14.

Regular Army officer, played quadrangular cricket in Central India, 1930s. Played for Rugby CC.

Brother, W.H. Harris, played for W.

HARRIS, Dennis Frank – RHB RM
b. Birmingham, 18 April 1911; d. Moseley, Birmingham, 17 December 1959. Educated at King Edward's Grammar School, Camp Hill, Birmingham.

Debut 1946 v Glos., Bristol (only match – amateur). 2 runs, only innings.

Played for Moseley, Birmingham League.

HARRIS, Earlsdon Joseph – RHB RMF
b. Lodge Village, St Kitts, W. Indies, 3 November 1952. Educated at Queensbridge Road Secondary Modern

School, Birmingham.

Debut 1975 v Oxford U, Oxford 1975. 4 matches for W 1975. Highest score: W 16 v Lancs., Old Trafford 1975. Best bowling: W 3–66 v Kent, Edgbaston 1975.

Played for Mitchells & Butlers, Moseley and Smethwick, all in Birmingham League.

HARRIS, William Henry – RHB WK
b. Rugby, 13 December 1883; d. Shabani, S. Rhodesia, 14 October 1967. Educated at Rugby School.

Debut 1904 v London County, Coventry and North W. 12 matches for W 1904–19 (amateur). Highest score: W 42 v Yorks., Edgbaston 1919.

Played for Rugby CC and Moseley (Birmingham League).

Amateur soccer, West Bromwich Albion.

Brother, A.J. Harris, played for W.

HAWKINS, Christopher George – RHB WK
b. Slough, Bucks., 31 August 1938.

Debut 1957 v Cambridge U, Edgbaston. 4 matches for W 1957 (professional). Highest score: W 11* v Northants, Northampton 1957.

Played for Bucks., 1956, 1965; Mitchells & Butlers and Old Hill in Birmingham League; also Pickwick CC.

Became a groundsman, holding position of head groundsman at Old Trafford for several years until 1983.

1988; best bowling 6–68 v Notts., Dore 1986.

HARGREAVE, Sam – LHB SLA
b. Rusholme, Manchester, 22 September 1875; d. Stratford-upon-Avon, 1 January 1929.

Debut 1899 v Australia, Edgbaston. 188 matches for W 1899–1909 (professional – capped). Highest score: W 45 v Leics., Leicester 1907. Best bowling: W 9–35 (15–76 match) v Surrey, The Oval 1903. 100 wickets (5); 128 (12.82) 1903 best. Played for Players v Gentlemen three times.

Toured Australia and New Zealand with Lord Hawke's Team, 1902–03. 919 wickets (21.84) in first-class career. Played for Stratford-upon-Avon.

Contract cancelled 1909 due to disciplinary problems. Later career troubled by muscular injury in shoulder.

HARTLEY, Peter John – RHB RMF
b. Keighley, Yorks., 18 April 1960. Educated at Greenhill Grammar School, Bradford College.

Debut 1982 v Lancs., Edgbaston. 3 matches for W 1982. Highest score: W 16 v Lancs., Southport 1982. Best bowling: W 2–45 v Yorks., Leeds 1982.

Played for Yorks. since 1985 (cap 1987); highest score 127* v Lancs., Old Trafford

HARVEY, William Henry Tomkins – RHB RM
b. Freemantle, Southampton, 12 April 1896. Educated at Aldershot.

Debut 1927 v Leics., Leicester (only match – amateur) 24 in only innings.

Played for Border in Currie Cup 1920–21, and for Mitchells & Butlers in Birmingham League.

Played League soccer for Sheffield Wednesday and Birmingham, and won

England Amateur International caps. Became Assistant Manager of Birmingham FC, and Manager of Chesterfield and Gillingham. Resigned as Gillingham FC Manager in July 1939 and in an interview with the *Kent Messenger* he stated that he would be staying in Association Football but first needed a holiday. So far as is known, *he has not been heard of from that day to this.*

HASTILOW, Cyril Alexander Frederick – RHB RA Spin
b. Birmingham, 31 May 1895; d. Moseley, Birmingham, 30 September 1975. Educated at Central Grammar School, Birmingham.
Debut 1919 v Surrey, Edgbaston. 2 matches for W 1919 (amateur). Highest score: W 14 v Worcs., Edgbaston 1919. Best bowling: W 2–56 same match. W Committee 1933–47; 1963–66; Committee Chairman 1948–62.
Played for Moseley (Birmingham League) and Harborne.
Awarded CBE for services to industry in Birmingham.
Daughter married A.H. Kardar (W, India, Pakistan).

C.A.F. Hastilow, chairman (1948–62)

HAYHURST, Albert – RHB RFM
b. Birdwell, Yorks., 17 July 1905.
Educated at Birdwell School.
  Debut 1934 v Kent, Tunbridge Wells. 7
matches for W 1934–35 (professional).
Highest score: W 42 v Surrey, Portland
Road 1934. Best bowling: W 4–120 v Kent,
Edgbaston 1934.
  Played for Bucks. 1948–53. Professional
with Coventry Colliery (Coventry
League).
  Soccer for Reading, Luton Town.

HEATH, David Michael William – RHB
b. Birmingham, 14 December 1931.
Educated at Moseley Grammar School.
  Debut 1949 v Combined Services,
Edgbaston, with one year left at school. 16
matches for W 1949–53 (amateur). Highest
score: W 54 v Northants, Edgbaston 1950.
W Committee 1981–86; W General
Secretary since 1986.
  Scored 149, Combined Services v
Worcs., Worcester 1952. Played for

Moseley (Birmingham League) 1947–69,
becoming captain and, latterly, President.

**HELLAWELL, Michael Stephen – RHB
RM**
b. Keighley, Yorks., 30 June 1938.
  Debut 1962 v Oxford U, Edgbaston
(only match – amateur). Highest score: W
30*. Best bowling: W 4–54.
  Played for Walsall (Birmingham
League), Keighley, Crossflatts.
  Played soccer (wing forward) for
Queen's Park Rangers, Birmingham,
Sunderland, Huddersfield, Peterborough
and England (2 caps).

**HEMMINGS, Edward Ernest – RHB
RM/OB**
b. Leamington Spa, 20 February 1949.
Educated at Campion School, Leamington
Spa.
  Debut 1966 v Scotland, Edgbaston, 177
matches for W 1966–78 (cap 1974). Highest
score: W 85 v Essex, Edgbaston 1977. Best
bowling: W 7–33 v Cambridge U,
Cambridge 1975. Achieved hat trick v
Worcs., Edgbaston 1977.

Joined Notts. 1979 – still playing 1988 season. Benefit 1987. Highest first-class score 127* Notts. v Yorkshire, Worksop 1982. Best first-class bowling 10–175 International XI v W. Indian XI, Kingston 1982–83. 5 Test matches for England 1982–83: 198 runs (22.00), 12 wickets (46.50).

HEWETSON, Edward Pearson – RHB RF
b. Birmingham, 27 May 1902; d. Brampton, Oxon., 26 December 1977. Educated at Shrewsbury and Pembroke College, Oxford.

Debut 1919 v Worcs., Edgbaston (still had two full years at school). 29 matches for W 1919–27 (amateur). Highest score: W 37* v Australia, Edgbaston 1926. Best bowling: W 5–31 v Derby., Edgbaston 1924.

Played for Oxford U 1922–25 (Blue 1923–25); 1213 runs (14.44) and 163 wickets (25.58) in first-class career. Played for West Bromwich Dartmouth (Birmingham League), Windermere CC.

Teacher at St Edward's, Oxford (recommended Peter Cranmer to W) and later prep. school proprietor in Cumberland. Athletics Blue at Oxford, and played hockey for Oxon.

HEWITT, Eric Joseph – RHB LB
b. Erdington, Birmingham, 19 December 1935. Educated at Coleshill Grammar School.

Debut 1954 v Oxford U, Edgbaston (only match). Highest score: W 40.

1 match for Combined Services 1957. Played for Aston Unity (Birmingham League), King's Heath, Solihull.

Became professional motor-racing driver.

HICKMAN, George – RHB
b. Burnopfield, Co. Durham, 19 January 1909; d. Stranraer, Scotland, 26 August 1978.

Debut 1929 v Derby., Edgbaston. 2 matches for W 1929 (professional). Highest score: W 17 v Kent, Tunbridge Wells 1929.

Played 2 matches for Minor Counties 1935. Played for West Bromwich Dartmouth (Birmingham League), Coventry Colliery and various teams in Yorks. and Durham.

Soccer player, West Bromwich Albion and Halifax Town.

HILDITCH, Thomas Arthur – RHB RFM
b. Sandbach, Cheshire, 10 January 1885; d.

Attleborough, Nuneaton, 7 August 1957.

Debut 1907 v Northants, Edgbaston. 8 matches for W 1907–13 (amateur). Highest score: W 17 v Hants, Southampton 1907. Best bowling: W 3–41 v Glos., Nuneaton CC 1913.

Played for Nuneaton, Foleshill Albion, Attleborough and Rover in Coventry League.

Soccer (goalkeeper) for Nuneaton and Aston Villa.

HILL, Alfred John (known as Bostock-Hill) – RHB
b. Olton, Solihull, 8 April 1887; d. Okehampton, Devon, 20 August 1959. Educated at Birmingham U.

Debut 1920 v Surrey, Edgbaston (only match – amateur). Highest score: W 4.

Played for Sparkhill and Olton.

Uncles, H.G.B. Hill and J.E. Hill both played for W.

HILL, Geoffrey Harold – LHB SLA
b. Halesowen, Worcs., 17 September 1934. Educated at Handsworth Technical College, Birmingham.

Debut 1958 v Leics., Edgbaston 1958. 41 matches for W 1958–60 (professional). Highest score: W 23 v Worcs., Edgbaston 1958. Best bowling: W 8–70 v Glos., Cheltenham 1958.

Played for Dudley and Stourbridge (Birmingham League) and King's Heath.

HILL, Henry Barratt Grosvenor – RHB LM

b. Old Square, Birmingham, 23 July 1861; d. Handsworth, Birmingham, 4 June 1913. Educated at King Edward's School, Birmingham.

Debut 1894 v Notts., Trent Bridge. Played for W pre-first-class cricket from 1890. 5 matches for W 1894–1900 (amateur). Highest score: W 13 v Yorks., Bradford 1895. Best bowling: W 3–15 v Glos., Edgbaston 1894. W Committee 1891–1912.

Founder and First Hon. Sec., Birmingham and District League 1888–1909. Played in Birmingham League Cricket for Handsworth Wood.

Brother, J.E. Hill, and nephew, A.J. Bostock-Hill, played for W.

HILL, John Ernest – RHB

b. Birmingham, 22 September, 1867; d. Smethwick, 2 December 1963. Educated at King Edward's School, Birmingham.

Warwickshire 1894 v Notts., Trent Bridge (played pre-first-class from 1890). 25 matches for W 1894–98 (amateur). Highest score: W 139* on debut. (First W batsman to score century on first-class debut.)

Played for Handsworth Wood (Birmingham League).

A solicitor who became Crown Prosecutor for Birmingham.

Brother, H.B.G. Hill, and nephew, A.J. Bostock-Hill, played for W.

HILL, William Aubrey – RHB RM

b. Carmarthen, S. Wales, 27 April 1910. Educated at Edgwick School, Coventry.

Debut 1929 v Som., Taunton. 169 matches for W 1929–48 (amateur until 1931, then professional – cap 1933). Highest score: W 147* v Northants, Edgbaston 1936. 1000 runs (2); 1197 (24.42) 1947 best.

Played for Foleshill Albion (Coventry League).

Coach at Oxford U during 1960s.

HITCHCOCK, Raymond Edward – LHB RLB
b. Christchurch, New Zealand, 28 November 1929. Educated at West Christchurch High School.

Debut 1949 v Combined Services, Edgbaston. 319 matches for W 1949–64 (professional to 1956; amateur 1957–59; then professional – cap 1951). Benefit (£6,410) 1963. Highest score: W 153* v Derby., Chesterfield 1962. Best bowling: W 7–76 v Scotland, Edgbaston 1959. 1000 runs (5); 1695 (34.59) 1955 best. Chairman, W cricket committee, 1980–84.

Played once for Canterbury (NZ) 1947–48. 12442 runs (27.89); 194 wickets (29.63) first-class career record. Played for Knowle and Dorridge.

Rugby Union for Nuneaton, N. Midlands.

HODGSON, Geoffrey Dean – RHB
b. Carlisle, Cumberland, 22 October 1966. Educated at Nelson Thomlinson County School, Wigton; Loughborough University.

Debut 1987 v Sussex, Hove (Refuge Assurance Sunday League). Did not appear in a first-class match.

Played for Cumberland since 1984.

HOFFMAN, Dean Stewart – RHB RMF
b. Birmingham, 13 January 1966.

Educated at Moor End Lane School, Sutton Coldfield.

Debut 1985 v Surrey, Edgbaston. 17

matches for W 1985. Highest score: W 13*
on debut. Best bowling: W 4–100 v Notts.,
Nuneaton 1985.

1 match for Northants 1988. Played for
Moseley (Birmingham League).

innings.

Played first-class cricket (2) for MCC
1908–09. Played for, and organised,
Farnborough CC (W).

HOGG, William – RHB RFM
b. Ulverston, Cumbria, 12 July 1955.
Educated at Ulverston School.

Debut 1981 v Yorks., Edgbaston 50
matches for W 1981–83. Highest score: W
31 v Hants, Edgbaston 1981. Best bowling:
W 5–63 v Kent, Edgbaston 1983.

Played 44 matches for Lancs. 1976–80.
222 wickets (28.99) first-class career
record. Best bowling: 7–84, Lancs. v
Warwickshire, Old Trafford 1978.

Father-in-law, S. Ramadhin (W. Indies
and Lancs.).

HOLBECH, William Hugh – RHB
b. Montreal, Canada, 18 August 1882; d.
of wounds received in action at
Kruiseecke, Belgium, 1 November 1914 in
England. Educated at Eton.

Debut 1910 v Hants, Edgbaston (only
match – amateur). Did not score, either

HOLDSWORTH, Romilly Lisle – RHB
b. Mysore, S. India 25 February 1899; d.
Blagdon Hill, Somerset, 20 June 1976.

Eric Hollies takes his 2000th wicket in first-class cricket – that of Dews of Worcestershire (11 May 1955)

Educated at Repton and Magdalen College, Oxford.

Debut 1919 v Derby., Edgbaston. 30 matches for W 1919–21 (amateur). Highest score: W 141 v Worcs., Edgbaston 1920.

Oxford Blue 1919–22. 36 Matches Sussex 1925–29. Played N. India, and NWFP in Ranji Trophy 1934–35 to 1941–42. 4716 runs (26.20) in first-class career. Scored 202* Oxford U v Free Foresters 1921.

Was Headmaster, Doon School, Dehra Dun, India.

HOLLIES, William Eric – RHB LBG
b. Old Hill, Staffs., 5 June 1912; d. Chinley, Derby., 16 April 1981. Educated at Halesowen Grammar School.

Debut 1932 v Sussex, Edgbaston. 476 Matches for W 1932–57 (professional – cap 1933). Benefit (£4,897) 1948; Testimonial (£1,796) 1954. Highest score: W 47 v Sussex, Edgbaston 1954. Best bowling: W 10–49 v Notts., Edgbaston 1946 (7 bowled, 3 lbw). 100 wickets (14); 180 (15.14) 1946 best (both W records). 2201 wickets (20.45) for W – county record.

13 Tests for England 1934–35 to 1950; best Test bowling 7–50 v W. Indies, Georgetown 1934–35. 44 wickets (30.27 in Tests); 2323 wickets (20.94) in first-class cricket. Played Staffs. 1958. Played for Mitchells & Butlers, Old Hill, West Bromwich Dartmouth in Birmingham League.

Autobiography, *I'll Spin You a Tale*, 1955.

HOLLOWAY, Piran Christopher Laity – LHB WK

b. Helston, Cornwall, 1 October 1970. Educated at Taunton School.

Debut 1988 v Worcs., Edgbaston (with a further year remaining at school). Highest score: W 16 v Glam., Edgbaston 1988.

Plays for Mitchells & Butlers (Birmingham League) and Helston CC.

HOPKINS, David Charles – RHB RM
b. Birmingham, 11 February 1957. Educated at Moseley Grammar School.

Debut 1977 v Leics., Edgbaston. 36 matches for W 1977–81. Highest score: W 34* v Essex, Edgbaston 1979. Best bowling: W 6–67 v Somerset, Taunton 1982.

Played for Bucks. 1982. Birmingham League Cricket for West Bromwich Dartmouth.

HOPKINS, Frank Jesse – LHB LM
b. Kings Norton, Birmingham, 30 June 1875; d. Southampton, 16 January 1930.

Debut 1898 v Lancs., Liverpool. 11 matches for W 1898–1903 (professional). Highest score: W 13 v Essex, Leyton 1900. Best bowling: W 5–10 v Kent, Edgbaston 1898.

Assistant groundsman Edgbaston 1892–98; appointed groundsman at Southampton 1904. Played 3 matches for Hants 1906–11.

Career blighted when 'no-balled' for

throwing by umpire V.A. Titchmarsh v Kent, Tunbridge Wells 1898.

HORNER, Norman Frederick – RHB
b. Queensbury, Yorks., 10 May 1926.

Debut 1951 v Scotland, Edgbaston. 357 matches for W 1951–65 (professional – cap 1953). Benefit (£6,465) 1962. Highest W 203* v Surrey, The Oval 1960 (adding 377 with Khalid Ibadulla – W 1st wicket record). 1000 runs (12); 1902 (33.36) 1960 best.

2 matches for Yorks. 1950. 18533 runs (29.79) in first-class career.

Became sportsfield groundsman after retirement. An outstanding outfielder with speed and fine throw.

HOSSELL, John Johnson – LHB SLA
b. Birmingham, 25 May 1914. Educated at Wylde Green College, Birmingham.

Debut 1939 v Cambridge U, Edgbaston 1939. 35 matches for W 1939–47 (amateur – cap 1946). Highest score: W 83 v Leics., Edgbaston 1946. Best bowling: W 3–24 v Cambridge U, Edgbaston 1947.

Played for Aston Unity (Birmingham League), Stratford-upon-Avon.

HOUGHTON, William Eric – RHB RM
b. Billingborough, Lincs., 29 June 1910.

Educated at Donnington Grammar School.

Debut 1946 v India, Edgbaston. 7 matches for W 1946–47 (amateur). Highest score: W 41 v Northants, Edgbaston 1947.

Played for Lincs. 1932–39; and for Aston Unity (Birmingham League), Sleaford, Olton.

A famous footballer playing for England (7 caps), Aston Villa (392 matches) and Notts County, managing both clubs.

HOWELL, Albert Louis – RHB RMF
b. Ladywood, Birmingham, 26 July 1898; d. Wingrove, Newcastle-on-Tyne, 26 July 1958. Educated at Dudley Road School, Birmingham.

Debut 1919 v Worcs., Edgbaston. 34 matches for W 1919–22 (professional). Highest score: W 26 v Kent, Dover 1921. Best bowling: W 5–65 v Middlesex, Lord's 1921.

Played for Minor Counties XI v Lancs., Old Trafford 1929. Played for Durham 1926–36. Professional for South Shields.

Coach at Uppingham. Brother, Harry Howell, (played for W and England).

HOWELL, Henry ('Harry') – RHB RF
b. Hockley, Birmingham, 29 December 1890; d. Selly Oak, Birmingham, 9 July 1932. Educated at Dudley Road School.

Debut 1913 v Yorks., Edgbaston 198 matches for W 1913–28 (professional – capped 1914). Benefit (£804) 1924. Highest score: W 36 v Yorks., Hull 1923. Best bowling: W 10–51 v Yorks., Edgbaston

1923 (first Warwickshire bowler to take all 10 wickets). Match analysis 14–71 v Somerset, Taunton 1924. 100 wickets (6); 152 (19.92) 1923 best.

5 Tests for England 1920–21 to 1924–25; 7 wickets (79.85) 975 wickets (21.23) in first-class career. Played for Aston Unity (Birmingham League).

League soccer for Wolves, Port Vale, Stoke City.

Brother, Albert Howell, played for W.

HUMPAGE, Geoffrey William – RHB WK RM
b. Sparkhill, Birmingham, 24 April 1954.

*Geoff Humpage became the highest-scoring wicketkeeper-batsman for
Warwickshire in 1988*

Educated at Golden Hillock School, Birmingham.

Debut 1974 v Oxford U, Oxford. 309 matches for W 1974–date (cap 1976). Benefit (information not yet available) 1987. Highest score: W 254 v Lancs., Southport 1982 – adding 470 for 4th wicket with Alvin Kallicharran English and W record for 4th wicket and highest stand for any wicket for a losing side. Best bowling: W 2–13 v Glos., Edgbaston 1980. 1000 runs (10); 1891 (48.48) 1984 best. 80 dismissals (W record) 1985. More runs for W than any other wicketkeeper.

Toured S. Africa with SABXI 1981–82, bringing England ban. Orange Free State in 1981–82.

HYDE, Alfred Joseph – LHB SLA
b. *c* 1884. No further details known.

Debut 1905 v Northants, Northampton. 2 matches for W 1905–07 (professional). Highest score: W 2* on debut. Best bowling: W 1–22 on debut.

I

ILLINGWORTH, Edward Arnold – LHB SLA

b. Dewsbury, Yorks., 1896; d. Barnsley, Yorks., 2 April 1924.

Debut 1920 v Oxford U, Oxford. 6 matches for W 1920 (professional).

Highest score: W 8* v Surrey, The Oval 1920. Best bowling: W 2–18 v Oxford U, Oxford 1920.

Played for King's Heath 1920; Great Horton Methodists, Idle Baptists after leaving W.

JACKSON, Arnold Kenneth – RHB RFM
b. Edgbaston, 21 June 1903; d. Halstenbeck, W. Germany, 31 May 1971.

Debut 1928 v Notts., Trent Bridge. 2 matches for W 1928–31 (amateur). Highest score: W 3* v Kent, Portland Road 1931. W Committee 1959–71.

Played for Harborne CC.

JAMESON, John Alexander – RHB RM/OB occ. WK
b. Bombay, India, 30 June 1941. Educated at Taunton School.

Debut 1960 v Oxford U, Portland Road. 345 matches for W 1960–76 (professional – cap 1964). Benefit (£13,500) 1974. Highest score: W 240* v Glos., Edgbaston 1974. Best bowling: W 4–22 v Oxford U, Oxford 1971. 1000 runs (11); 1948 (48.70) 1973 best. Added 465 (unbroken) with R. Kanhai, v Glos., Edgbaston during best innings above – world and W 2nd wicket record, and highest unbroken stand in English first-class cricket. Scored 103 before lunch in last first-class innings, v Glam., Edgbaston 1976. Also 100* before lunch, 1st day of match v Hants at Bournemouth, same season. Achieved hat trick v Glos., Edgbaston 1965.

Played for Smethwick (Birmingham League); 4 Tests for England 1971 to 1973–74. 214 runs (26.75). Highest score 82 v India, The Oval 1971. 18941 runs (33.34) in first-class cricket.

First-class umpire 1984–87; Sussex coach 1987–88. Appointed Assistant Secretary of MCC in 1989. Brother, Tom Jameson, played for W.

JAMESON, Thomas Edward Neville – LHB RMF
b. Bombay, India, 23 July 1946. Educated at Taunton School, Durham U, Emmanuel College, Cambridge.

Debut 1970 v Cambridge U, Edgbaston (only match). Highest score: W 32 on debut.

91

Cambridge Blue 1970. Plays for Knowle & Dorridge.
Brother, John Jameson, played for W.

JARRETT, Harold Harvey – RHB LBG
b. Johannesburg, S. Africa 23 September 1907; d. Newport, Gwent, 17 March 1983.

Debut 1932 v India, Edgbaston. 14 matches for W 1932–33 (professional). Highest score: W 45 on debut. Best bowling: W 8–187 v Leics., Hinckley 1932.

1 match for Glam. 1938. Became professional in Scotland and Wales.

Editor, *South Wales Cricketers'*

Magazine 1948–51. Son, Keith Jarrett, cricket for Glam., Rugby Union for Wales, British Lions, Newport; Rugby League for Great Britain.

JEEVES, Percy – RHB RMF
b. Earlsheaton, Yorks., 5 March 1888; d. High Wood, Montauban, France (in action), 22 July 1916.

Debut 1912 v Australia, Edgbaston. 49 matches for W 1912–14 (professional – cap 1913). Highest score for W 86* v Yorks., Edgbaston 1913. Best bowling: W 7–34 v Worcs., Edgbaston 1913. 106 wickets (20.88) in 1913.

Played for Moseley (Birmingham League), Hawes, Goole.

Was P.G. Wodehouse's model for Jeeves.

JENNINGS, George Adolphus – RHB SLA
b. The Friars, Exeter, Devon, 14 January 1895; d. Marlborough, Wilts., July 1959.

Debut 1923 v W. Indies, Edgbaston 1923. 20 matches for W 1923–25 (professional). Highest score: W 41 on debut. Best bowling: W 5–92 v S. Africa, Edgbaston 1924.

Played for Devon 1920–22.

Later Coach at Marlborough until 1959. Father, D.J. Jennings played for Devon

and coached at Marlborough College; Brothers, D.W. (Kent), L.F. (RAF) and T.S. (Surrey), all played first-class cricket.

JONES, Alan Keith Colin – RHB
b. Solihull, 20 April 1951. Educated at Solihull School and St Edmund Hall, Oxford.

Debut 1969 v Scotland, Edgbaston (while still one year to do at school). 4 matches for W 1969–73. Highest score: W 62 v Kent, Edgbaston 1973. Oxford Blue 1971–73 – captain in 1973. Highest first-class score 111 v Notts., Oxford 1971; 1403 runs (21.92) in first-class career.

Played for Solihull CC.

JONES, Richard Henry (now R.H. Cartwright-Jones) – LHB RM
b. Redditch, Worcs., 3 November 1916. Educated at Aston Commercial School, Birmingham.

Debut 1946 v Som., Edgbaston (only match – amateur). Highest score: W 23.

Played for Mitchells & Butlers (Birmingam League), King's Heath, Ombersley, Newport (Mon).

K

XIs 1982–83 and 1983–84; subsequently barred for life from W. Indian cricket. 1000 runs (11); 2301 runs (52.29) 1984 best. Added 470 for 4th wicket with Geoff Humpage v Lancs., Southport 1982; best stand for any wicket other than the first in English first-class cricket; English and W 4th wicket record and highest stand anywhere for a losing side. Played club cricket for Rugby.

Classed as 'Englishman' for qualification purposes in 1988.

KALLICHARRAN, Alvin Isaac – LHB ROB
b. Paidama, British Guiana (Guyana), 21 March 1949. Educated at Port Mourant School.

Debut 1971 v Pakistan, Edgbaston. 262 matches for W 1971–date (cap 1972). Benefit (£34,097) 1983. Highest score: W 243* v Glam., Edgbaston 1983. Best bowling: W 4–48 v Derby., Edgbaston 1978.

Best first-class bowling – 5–45, Transvaal v W. Province, Cape Town 1982–83. Played for Guyana 1966–67 to 1980–81; Queensland 1977–78; Transvaal 1981–82 to 1983–84; Orange Free State 1984–85 to date. 66 Test matches for W. Indies 1971–72 to 1980–81; 4399 runs (44.43) 12 centuries. W. Indies captain 9 times. Highest Test score 187 v India, Bombay 1978–79. Toured S. Africa with W. Indian

KANHAI, Rohan Babulal – RHB occ. WK
b. Port Mourant, Berbice, British Guiana (Guyana), 26 December 1935. Educated at Port Mourant School.

Debut 1968 v Cambridge U, Cambridge (scoring 119). 173 matches for W 1968–77 (cap 1968). Benefit (£11,500) 1977. Highest score: W 253 v Notts., Trent Bridge 1968. 1000 runs (6) 1819 (46.64) 1968 best. Added 465 (unbeaten) with John Jameson v Glos., Edgbaston 1974;

world 2nd wicket record and highest partnership for any wicket in England. Career average of 51.62 for W is the highest ever.

Played for British Guiana (Guyana) 1954–55 to 1973–74; appeared in W. Australia 1961–62, Tasmania 1969–70. 79 Test matches for W. Indies, 1957 to 1973–74, 13 as captain. Test record 6227 runs, average 47.53. Highest Test score 256 v India, Calcutta 1958–59. Full first-class record; 28774 runs (49.01) 83 centuries. Played for numerous clubs as professional in N. England, Scotland and Australia.

Autobiographies: *Blasting for Runs* (1966) and *Blashing for Runs* (1970).

KARDAR, Abdul Hafeez – LHB SLA
b. Lahore, India, 17 January 1925. Educated at Islamia College, Punjab U and University College, Oxford.

Debut 1948 v Scotland, Edgbaston. 45 matches for W 1948–50 (amateur – cap 1949). Highest score W: 112 v Middlesex, Lord's 1950. Best bowling: W 5–25 v Leics., Coalville 1950.

Highest first-class score 173, N. Zone v Australian Services, Lahore 1945–46. Oxford Blue 1947–48–49. Best first-class bowling 7–25 N. India v Delhi, Lahore 1944–45. Played domestic cricket in India

for N. India and Bombay Muslims 1943–44 to 1945–46. Played in Pakistan for Parkistan Services. 3 Tests for India in 1946, then 23 Tests for Pakistan (all as captain) 1952–53 to 1957–58. Test record 927 runs (23.76); 21 wickets (45.42). Full first-class career record: 6814 runs (29.75); 344 wickets (24.55).

President, Board of Control for Cricket in Pakistan 1972–77. Married the daughter of C.A.F. Hastilow who played for W. Author of *Green Shadows* (1958).

KEMP-WELCH, George Durant – RHB RFM
b. London, 4 August 1907; d. in air raid on Guards Chapel, London, 18 June 1944. Educated at Charterhouse and Cambridge U.

Debut 1927 v Middx., Lord's 57 matches for W 1927–35 (amateur). Highest score: W 123* v Glam., Swansea 1934. Best bowling: W 2–45 v Worcs., Edgbaston 1929.

Cambridge U 1929–31 – Blue each season. Toured Jamaica with Tennyson's team 1931–32, obtaining career highest score 186 v All-Jamaica at Kingston. Best first-class bowling 4–41 Cambridge U v Surrey, The Oval 1929. 4172 first-class runs (24.82).

Gained Blue for soccer. Father-in-law was Rt Hon Stanley Baldwin, MP, one-time Prime Minister.

KENDALL, John Thomas – RHB WK
b. Hawkesbury, Coventry, 31 March 1921.
Educated at Foxford School, Coventry.

Debut 1948 v Oxford U, Oxford 1948. 4 matches for W 1948–49 (professional). Highest score: W 18* v Cambridge U, Cambridge 1949.

Played for various clubs, Coventry League. Soccer, Coventry City.

KENNEDY, John Maxwell – RHB
b. Manchester, 15 December 1931. Educated at Urmston Grammar School; Loughborough College.

Debut 1960 v Oxford U, Portland Road. 31 matches for W 1960–62 (professional). Highest score: W 94 v Oxford U,

Edgbaston 1962. Took 2–1 in only bowl in first-class cricket, v Somerset, Edgbaston 1960.

Played for Aston Unity (Birmingham League); Lightcliffe (Bradford).

KENT, Kenneth Gwynne – RHB RMF
b. Moseley, Birmingham, 10 December 1901; d. Fife, Scotland, 29 December 1974. Educated at King Edward's, Birmingham.

Debut 1927 v Lancs., Edgbaston. 9 matches for W 1927–31 (amateur). Highest score: W 23*v Hants, Bournemouth 1928. Best bowling: W 3–91 v Lancs., Edgbaston 1927 (debut).

Played for Moseley (Birmingham League); also Harborne, Leamington, Moseley Ashfield.

KERR, Kevin John – RHB OB
b. Airdrie, Scotland, 11 September 1961.

Educated at Sandown High School, S. Africa and Witwatersrand U.

Debut 1986 v Worcs., Edgbaston. 14 matches for W 1986. Highest score: W 45* v Glos., Nuneaton Griff & Coton 1986. Best bowling: W 5–47 v Glam. 1986.

Played for Transvaal and Transvaal B since 1978–79. 860 first-class runs (17.20) 165 wickets (28.43). Played for Moseley (Birmingham League).

Zealand) 1964–65 to 1966–67. Tasmania 1970–71 to 1971–72. 4 Tests for Pakistan 1964–65 to 1967 – scored 166 v Australia, Karachi, 1964–65 on Test debut. 253 Test runs (31.62). 17039 first-class runs (27.30); 462 wickets (30.87).

First-class umpire 1982–83; subsequently coach in Otago, New Zealand. Son, K.B.K. Ibadulla, plays for Glos. and Otago.

KHALID IBADULLA ('Billy') – RHB RM OB

b. Lahore (then India, now Pakistan) 20 December 1935. Educated at Manzang High School, Lahore.

Debut 1954 v Oxford U, Edgbaston. 377 matches for W 1954–72 (professional – cap 1957). Benefit (£7,797) 1969. Highest score: W 171 v Oxford U, Oxford 1961. Best bowling: W 7–22 v Derby., Chesterfield 1967. 1000 runs (6); 2098 (33.83) 1962 best. Added 377 unbeaten, with Norman Horner v Surrey, The Oval 1960; County 1st wicket record and highest unbroken first wicket stand in English first-class cricket.

Played Pakistan Domestic Cricket (Punjab XI) 1953–54. Played for Otago (N.

KILNER, Norman – RHB RM/LM

b. Low Valley, Wombwell, Yorks., 21 July 1895; d. Alum Rock, Birmingham, 28 April 1979. Educated at Wombwell. C of E school.

Debut 1924 v S. Africa, Edgbaston. 330 matches for W 1924–37 (professional – cap 1926). Benefit (£778) 1937. Highest score: W 228 v Worcs., Worcester 1935. Best bowling: W 1–19 v Kent, Tunbridge Wells 1926. 1000 runs (12); 2114 (45.96) 1933 best.

Played for Yorks. 1919–23. First-class career record: 17522 runs (30.36); 25 centuries. Played for West Bromwich Dartmouth (Birmingham League).

First-class umpire 1938, 1946; coach and groundsman at Edgbaston 1939–45; coach and groundsman, Birmingham U 1946–65. Brother, Roy Kilner (Yorks. and England); uncle, Irving Washington (Yorks., Griqualand West, Transvaal).

Billy Ibadulla (left) *and Bob Barber take the field in the 1966 Gillette Cup Final match against Worcestershire at Lord's*

KING, Edmund Hugh – RHB OB
b. Edgbaston, 26 March 1906; d. Cropthorne, Worcs. after motor accident, 25 November 1981. Educated at Ampleforth.

Debut 1928 v Sussex, Edgbaston. 7 matches for W 1928–32 (amateur). Highest score: W 24 on debut. W Committee 1936–81; Committee Chairman 1962–72.

Played for Harborne, Knowle & Dorridge.

Harborne, and England trial (hockey). Chairman, TCCB Finance and General Purposes Sub-committee 1968–80.

KING, Ian Metcalfe – LHB SLA
b. Leeds, Yorks., 10 November 1931.

Educated at Hanley Castle Grammar School, Worcester.

Debut 1952 v Kent, Maidstone. 53 matches for W 1952–55. Highest score: W 29* v Glam., Llanelly 1954. Best bowling: W 5–59 v Essex, Ilford 1954.

28 games for Essex 1957. First-class record: 128 wickets (28.95). Played in Birmingham League for Aston Unity, Kidderminster, Moseley.

Cousin, Anthony King, played for Yorks.

KINGSTON, James Phillips – RHB LB
b. Northampton, 8 July 1857; d. in Italy, 14 March 1929. Educated at Abingdon House School, Northampton.

Debut 1894 v Leics., Leicester 1894 (only match – amateur). 24 in only innings.

Played for Northants 1875–93 (Captain 1877–87, 1891; Hon. Secretary 1892–93).

Brothers, F.W. Kingston (Cambridge U), C.A. Kingston (British Guiana), H.E. and W.H. Kingston (Northants).

KINNEIR, Septimus 'Paul' – LHB SLA
b. Corsham, Wilts., 13 May 1871; d. Hall Green, Birmingham, 16 October 1928 (found dead on the road next to his motor cycle, returning home from playing golf. Death was from natural causes).

Debut 1898 v Derby., Derby. 302 matches for W 1898–1914 (professional –

capped. 1900 or 1901). Benefit (£467) 1914. Highest score: W 268* v Hants, Edgbaston 1911 (record for W at the time; remains record for W left-hander). Best bowling: W 3–13 v Leics., Edgbaston 1900. 1000 runs (7); 1521 (41.10) 1905 best. Scored 124 and 110 in match v Sussex, Chichester 1911 – first W player to obtain two separate centuries in a match. Carried bat through innings 3 times; 70 out of 239 and 69 out of 166 v Leics., Leicester 1907 – only W batsman to perform feat twice in same match – and 65 out of 164 v Som., Taunton 1908. Added 327 with Billy Quaife, v Lancs at Edgbaston 1901 – still W 3rd wicket record. 333 added with Fred Byrne v Lancs., Edgbaston 1905 1st wicket record until 1960.

One Test v Australia (Sydney) 1911–12, scoring 22 and 30. First-class record: 15641 runs (32.72); 26 centuries. Played for Wilts. before joining W; Birmingham League cricket for Handsworth Wood; also played for Stratford-upon-Avon and Sparkhill Belvedere.

KIRK, Edwin – RHB

b. Coventry, 6 May 1866; d. Coventry, 10 March 1957.

Debut 1898 v Derby., Edgbaston (only match 1898). Scored 0 in only innings.

Played for Mitchells & Butlers (Birmingham League), Coventry and North W.

Related to A.R. West (Leics.).

KIRTON, Harold Osborne – RHB RM

b. London, 4 January 1894; d. Holland-on-Sea, Essex, 9 May 1974. Educated at London Council School.

Debut 1925 v Surrey, Edgbaston. 2 matches for W 1925–29 (amateur). Highest score: W 52 v Middx., Lord's 1929.

Played very successfully for Mitchells & Butlers (Birmingham League).

Played very successfully for Mitchells & Butlers (Birmingham League).

KNUTTON, Herbert John ('Jack') – RHB RF

b. St Johns, Coventry, 14 June 1867; d. Bradford, 12 December 1946.

Debut 1894 v Notts., Edgbaston (only match). Scored 4 in only innings; 0 wickets.

Played for England XI v Australia at Bradford 1902, producing figures of 9–100 and 1–17. For many years a professional in northern England, taking over 1000 wickets for Bradford in the Bradford League.

Regarded as one of the fastest bowlers in England but doubts about his action hindered his progress in the first-class game. Became well-known sports outfitter in Bradford.

L

LANE, Albert Frederick ('Spinney') – RHB OB
b. Rowley Regis, Staffs., 29 August 1885; d. Upper Fulbrook, W, 29 January 1948. (Death from natural causes; erroneously attributed to car accident in some sources.)

Debut 1919 v Yorks., Edgbaston. 12 matches for W 1919–25 (amateur). Highest score: W 58 v Lancs., Edgbaston 1919. Best bowling: W 4–56 v Northants, Northampton 1919.

Played for Worcs 1914 (as professional), 1927–32 (as amateur). Played for Staffs. 1910. Debut for Stourbridge 1900 aged 14 (youngest player in Birmingham League). Later played for Aston Unity (Birmingham League), Ormskirk (professional).

In WWII helped organise cricket in Midlands.

LANGLEY, Colin Kendall – RHB RFM
b. Narborough, Leics., 11 July 1888; d. Leamington Spa, 26 June 1948. Educated at Radley and Hertford College, Oxford.

Debut 1908 v Northants, Edgbaston. 33

matches for W 1908–14. Highest score: W 61* v Middx., Edgbaston 1914. Best bowling: W 8–29 v Worcs., Edgbaston 1912. W Committee; 1919–43; Hon. Secretary 1943–48.

Played for Moseley (Birmingham League).

LATHAM, Hubert Joseph ('Bert') – RHB RF
b. Winson Green, Birmingham, 13 November 1932. Educated at Handsworth

107

Grammar School.

Debut 1955 v Combined Services, Edgbaston. 10 matches for W 1955–59 (amateur). Highest score: W 26 v Surrey, The Oval 1958. Best bowling: W 6–49 v Combined Services, Edgbaston 1958. Played for Moseley (Birmingham League) taking over 1000 wickets. W Committee 1973–88.

Forced to retire from first-class cricket due to knee trouble.

LAW, Alfred – RHB
b. Birmingham, 16 December 1862; d. Handsworth, Birmingham, 10 May 1919.

Debut 1894 v Notts., Trent Bridge (played non-first-class from 1885). 52 matches for W 1894–99 (professional); Benefit (£380) 1899. Highest score: W 89 v Yorks., Bradford 1895.

Played for Aston Unity, Small Heath, Mitchells & Butlers, all in Birmingham League.

Professional coach, Radley 1909–19.

LEACH, Clive William – RHB SLA
b. Bombay, India, 4 December 1934.

Debut 1955 v Cambridge U, Edgbaston. 39 matches: W 1955–58 (professional). Highest score: W 67 v Derby., Derby 1957.

Best bowling: W 3–19 v Combined Services, Portland Road 1957.

Played for Durham 1959–65; Bucks. 1966–70. Played variously for Kenilworth, Bishop Auckland, Amersham, High Wycombe.

LEADBEATER, Edric ('Eddie') – RHB LBG
b. Huddersfield, Yorks., 15 August 1927.

Debut 1957 v Cambridge U, Edgbaston. 27 matches for W 1957–58 (professional). Highest score: W 116 v Glam., Coventry, Courtaulds 1958. Best bowling: W 6–63 v Cambridge U, Cambridge 1958.

81 matches for Yorks. 1949–56; best bowling 8–83, Yorks. v Worcs., Worcester 1950. 2 Tests for England in India 1951–52. Full first-class record; 1548 runs (15.18); 289 wickets (27.49). Played 2 Tests but never won a county cap for either Yorks. or W; this is unique.

Played club cricket in Yorks until 60th year.

LEGARD, Edwin ('Eddie') – RHB WK
b. Barnsley, Yorks. 23 August 1935.

Debut 1962 v Cambridge U, Cambridge. 20 matches: W 1962–68 (cap 1963). Highest score: W 21 v Scotland, Edgbaston 1967.

Played for Barnsley CC.

LETHBRIDGE, Christopher ('Arthur') – RHB RM
b. Castleford, Yorks. 23 June 1961. Educated at Normanton Secondary Modern School.

Debut 1981 v Yorks., Edgbaston. 50 matches for W 1981–85. Highest score: W 87* v Som., Taunton 1982. Best bowling: W 5–68 v Glam., Cardiff 1982. Took wicket of G. Boycott (Yorks.) with first ball in first-class cricket.

Played for Camb. since 1986.

Club: Hanging Heaton, Eltofts.

LEWINGTON, Peter John – RHB OB
b. Finchampstead, Berks., 30 January 1950.

Debut 1970 v Cambridge U., Edgbaston. 69 matches: W 1970–76; 1982. Highest score: W 34 v Essex, Edgbaston 1973. Best bowling: W 7–52 v Worcs., Worcester 1975.

Played for Walsall (Birmingham League), Perth (W. Australia, N. Taranaki

(N. Zealand), Finchampstead. Toured S. Africa with D.H. Robins' Team 1972–73. Played for Berks. 1967–69; 1977–81; 1983–date.

LEWIS, Esmond Burman – RHB WK
b. Shirley, Solihull 5 January 1918; d. Dorridge, Solihull, 19 October 1983. Educated at Wellesbourne House School, Birmingham.

Debut 1949 v Oxford U, Edgbaston (made 9 dismissals – 8 caught, 1 stumped on debut; still W record for 1 match). 43 matches for W 1949–58 (amateur – cap 1951). Highest score: W 51 v Services, Edgbaston 1949. Played 3 times for

Gentlemen v Players at Lord's. W Committee 1958–83.

Played for Sparkhill, King's Heath, Knowle & Dorridge; became well-known local umpire.

LILLEY, Arthur Frederick Augustus ('Dick') – RHB WK RM
b. Holloway Head, Birmingham, 28 November 1866; d. Brislington, Bristol, 17 November 1929.

Debut 1894 v Notts., Trent Bridge (non-first-class from 1888). 321 matches 1894–1911 (professional – cap c 1890). Benefit (£850) 1901. Highest score: W 171 v Worcs., Worcester 1907. Best bowling: W 6–46 v Derby., Derby 1896. 1157 runs (35.06) 1895. 8 dismissals in match (all caught) twice; v MCC, Lord's 1896, v Kent, Edgbaston 1897.

35 Tests for England 1896–1909; 903 runs (20.52); 70 ct 22st. First-class record; 15597 runs (26.30); 16 centuries; 171 caught, 197 stumped. Made first-class debut for North v South, Edgbaston 1891. Played for Handsworth Wood, Smethwick (Birmingham League) and King's Heath.

Author: *Twenty-four Years of Cricket* (1912).

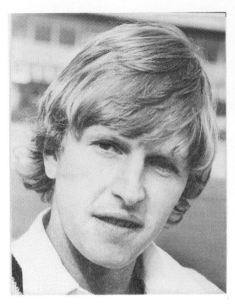

LLOYD, Timothy Andrew ('Andy') – LHB SRA
b. Oswestry, Salop. 5 November 1956. Educated at Oswestry High School and Dorset College of Higher Education.

Debut 1977 v Northants, Northampton. 217 matches for W 1977–date (cap 1980 – captain 1988–). Highest score: W 208* v Glos., Edgbaston 1983. Best bowling: 2–29 v India, Edgbaston 1982. 1000 runs (7); 1673 runs (45.22) 1983 best.

1 Test, England v W. Indies, Edgbaston 1984 – badly injured when struck on head by M.D. Marshall when 10* in first innings. Played for Orange Free State 1978–79 to 1979–80. Played for Salop 1975.

Clubs: Oswestry, Whittington, Bloemfontein Ramblers.

LOBB, Brian – RHB RFM
b. Birmingham, 11 January 1931. Educated at King Edward's School, Edgbaston; St Luke's College, Exeter.

Debut 1953 v Oxford U, Oxford (only match – professional). Best bowling: 2–31 in only innings.

Played 115 matches for Somerset 1955–69 (cap 1955). Highest first-class score 42 Som. v Yorks., Bath 1958. Best bowling first-class 7–43 Som. v Middx., Lord's 1957. Took 110 wickets (19.48)

1957. Played for Smethwick (Birmingham League), Harborne, Morlands. Became Som. Committee Member.

LORD, Gordon John – LHB SLA
b. Edgbaston, 25 April 1961. Educated at Warwick School, Durham U.
Debut 1983 v Notts., Trent Bridge. 18 matches for W 1983–86. Highest score: W

199 v Yorks., Edgbaston 1985. Played for Worcs. since 1986; played for Old Hill (Birmingham League).

LORD, William Alston – LHB LFM
b. Washwood Heath, Birmingham, 8 August 1873; d. Gravelly Hill, Erdington, 16 June 1906.
Debut 1897, v Surrey, Edgbaston. 13 matches for Warwickshire 1897–99 (professional). Highest score: W 10* v Yorks., Leeds 1898. Best bowling: W 5–73 v Glos., Gloucester 1897.
Played for Aston Unity and Mitchells & Butlers (Birmingham League).

LOVEITT, Frank Russell – LHB
b. Easenhall, Rugby, 24 April 1871; d. Coventry, 1 September 1939.
Debut 1898 v Leics., Leicester 1898. 25 matches for W 1898–1905 (amateur).

Highest score: W 110 v Glos., Edgbaston 1903.

Played for Coventry and North W, Leamington, Chilvers Coton.

Rugby Union three-quarter for Coventry.

LOWE, John Claude Malcolm – RHB RFM
b. Coventry, 21 February 1888; d. Hastings, Sussex, 27 July 1970. Educated at Uppingham and Oriel College, Oxford.

Debut 1907 v Hants, Edgbaston (only match; amateur). Highest score: W 8.

Played for Oxford U 1907–10; Blue 1907–09. Highest first-class score 46 Oxford U v Surrey, The Oval 1908. Best bowling first-class 8–144 Oxford U v Gentlemen, Eastbourne 1908. 106 first-class wickets (26.10).

Won Blue for hockey.

LOWE, Peter John – RHB WK
b. Sutton Coldfield, 7 January 1935; d.

Durdham Down, Bristol, August 1988 (his body was found at the bottom of the Avon Gorge).

Debut 1964 v Oxford U, Edgbaston 1964 (only match). Played for Sutton Coldfield.

LUCKIN, Verner Valentine – LHB RLBG
b. Maybury Hill, Woking, Surrey 14 February 1892; d. Froxfield, Hants, 28 November 1931.

Debut 1919 v Surrey, The Oval. 9 matches for W 1919 (professional). Highest score: W 59* v Lancs., Edgbaston 1919. Best bowling: W 3–19 v Derby., Edgbaston 1919.

10 matches for Hants 1910–12. First-class record: 212 runs (15.14); 24 wickets (35.20). Played for Moseley (Birmingham League).

LYNES, John – RHB RFM
b. Coleshill 6 June 1872. No details known of his death.

Debut 1898 v Lancs., Edgbaston. 8 matches for W 1898–1905 (professional). Highest score: W 26 v Surrey, Edgbaston 1904. Best bowling: W 3–54 v Worcs., Worcester 1904.

Became professional with various clubs in north of England.

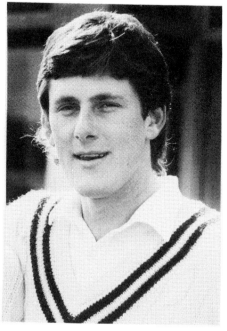

McDOWALL, James Ian ('Jamie') – RHB WK

b. Sutton Coldfield, 9 December 1947. Educated at Rugby School and Fitzwilliam College, Cambridge.

Debut 1969 v Som., Weston-super-Mare. 12 matches for W 1969–73. Highest score: W 89 v Oxford U, Oxford 1973. W Committee since 1973.

17 matches for Cambridge U 1969–70 (Blue 1969). First-class record 811 runs (16.89).

Clubs: Rugby Meteors, Knowle & Dorridge.

McMILLAN, Brian Mervin – RHB RMF

b. Welkom, Orange Free State, 22 December 1963. Educated at Carleton Jones High School and Witwatersrand U.

Debut 1986 v Essex, Edgbaston. 12 matches for W 1986. Highest score: W 136 v Notts., Trent Bridge 1986. Best bowling:

W 3–47 v Som., Weston-super-Mare 1986. Scored 999 runs (58.76) in his only season.

Played for Transvaal and Transvaal 'B' since 1984–85. Best first-class career record: 1903 runs (38.06); 79 wickets (28.59). Played for Moseley (Birmingham League).

McVICKER, Norman Michael – RHB RFM

b. Radcliffe, Lancs., 4 November 1940. Educated at Stand Grammar School, Manchester.

Debut v Cambridge U, Cambridge 1969. 104 matches: W 1969–73 (cap 1971). Highest score: W 65* v Lancs., Old Trafford 1972. Best bowling: W 7–29 v Northants, Edgbaston 1969.

Played for Leics. 1974–76 (cap 1973). Played 2 matches for Minor Counties

Debut 1982 v Northants, Northampton. 3 matches for W 1982. Highest score: W 2 v Somerset, Edgbaston 1982.

Played for Staffs. 1984; Moseley (Birmingham League) and Coleshill clubs.

MANTON, Joseph – RHB
b. West Bromwich, Staffs., 4 December 1871; d. Henham, Essex, 9 December 1958. Educated at King Edward's, Birmingham.

Debut 1898 v Surrey, The Oval (only match – amateur). Captained the side in his only first-class match. Scored 0 and 5, took 1–51.

Appeared for Handsworth Wood (Birmingham League).

1965–67. Highest first-class score 83* Leics. v Kent, Tunbridge Wells 1975. First-class record; 3108 runs (19.79); 453 wickets (25.53). Played for Lincs. 1963–68. Appeared for Solihull CC.

MARSHALL, Francis William – RHB
b. Rugby, 30 January 1888; d. Kensington, London, 24 May 1955. Educated at Rugby School.

Debut 1922 v Lancs., Old Trafford. 2 matches for W 1922 (amateur). Highest score: W 10 on debut.

Cricket for Olton CC.

MARSHALL, Gordon Alex – RHB RFM
b. Birmingham, 12 March 1935. Educated at King's Norton Grammar School, Birmingham.

Debut 1961 v Oxford U, Oxford. 4 matches for W 1961–63 (amateur).

Highest score: W 18* v Cambridge U, Portland Road 1961. Best bowling: W 5–22

MAGUIRE, Keith Robert – RHB RFM
b. Marston Green, W 20 March 1961. Educated at Sutton Coldfield Technical College.

at Warwick School.

Debut 1946 v Worcs., Dudley. 28 matches for W 1946–50 (amateur – cap 1946). Highest score: W 47 v Derby., Derby 1946 and v Glam., Edgbaston 1950. Best bowling: W 5–65 on debut.

1 match for MCC 1956. Played for Leamington CC.

Rugby Union for Nuneaton.

MATHESON, Edward – RHB occ. WK
b. Charlton, Kent, 14 June 1865; d. Uffculme, Tiverton, Devon, 26 February 1945. Educated at Clergy Orphan School, Canterbury.

Debut 1899 v Glos., Bristol (only match – amateur). Highest score: W 9.

One other first-class match, South v Australia, Hastings 1886.

A teacher at Summerfield School, St Leonards-on-Sea, usually played for Eastbourne, but a family residence in Leamington Spa qualified him for W when he also appeared for Leamington CC.

same match.

Played for King's Heath and Stratford-upon-Avon.

MARSHALL, John Maurice Alex – RHB LB
b. Kenilworth, 26 October 1916. Educated

MAUDSLEY, Ronald Harling – RHB RM
b. Lostock Gralam, Cheshire, 8 April 1918; d. San Diego, California, 29 September 1981. Educated at Malvern,

Birmingham U, Brasenose College, Oxford.

Debut 1946 v Glam., Edgbaston. 45 matches for W 1946–51 (amateur – cap 1946 – joint captain (with H.E. Dollery) 1948). Highest score: W 107 v Hants, Bournemouth 1949 and 107 v Oxford U, Stratford-upon-Avon 1951. Best bowling: W 6–54 v Surrey, The Oval 1946.

Played for Oxford U 1946–47 (Blue each season). Highest first-class score 130 Oxford U v Sussex, Chichester 1946.

Became a Professor of Law. Club: Harborne. Won Golf Blue.

MAYNARD, Christopher – RHB WK
b. Haslemere, Surrey, 8 April 1958. Educated at Bishop Vesey's Grammar School, Sutton Coldfield.

Debut 1978 v Lancs., Edgbaston. 24 matches for W 1978–82. Highest score: W 85 v Kent, Edgbaston 1979.

Moved to Lancs. 1982 appearing for them in County Championship the same season. Played for Lancs. 1982–86; contract cancelled 1988 due to knee injury. Highest first-class score 132* Lancs. v Yorks., Leeds 1986. Full first-class record: 2541 runs (20.65); 186 ct, 28 st.

MAYER, Joseph Herbert ('Danny') – RHB RFM
b. Audley, Staffs., 2 March 1902; d. Kingsbury, W, 6 September 1981. Educated at Kingsbury School.

Debut 1926 v Notts., Trent Bridge 332 matches for W 1926–39 (professional – cap 1926). Benefit (£509) 1933. Highest score: W 74* v Surrey, The Oval 1927 (added 126 with Bob Wyatt – at the time the County 10th wicket record; the 74* remains the highest score by a W no.11). Best bowling: W 8–62 v Surrey, Edgbaston 1928. 13–70 in match v Glos., Edgbaston 1937. 100 wickets (2); 126 (22.35) 1929 best.

Played in Birmingham League for Walsall.

MEAD-BRIGGS, Richard – RHB RFM/M
b. Sturry, Kent, 25 March 1902; d.

*The Warwickshire team inspect the pitch at Lord's two days before their 1964
Gillette Cup Final against Sussex*

Birmingham, 15 January 1956. Educated at
King's School, Canterbury.

Debut 1946 v Sussex, Edgbaston. 2
matches for W 1946 (amateur). Highest
score: 44* v Leics., Edgbaston 1946.

Played for Harborne CC.

MELDON, William Waltrude – RHB RM
b. Dublin, Ireland, 8 April 1879; d.
Putney, London, 23 May 1957. Educated
at Beaumont College.

Debut 1909 v Glos., Edgbaston. 5
matches for W 1909–10 (amateur). Highest
score: W 44 on debut. Best bowling: W
3–27 v Northants, Northampton 1909.

5 matches for Ireland 1911–14. Played
for Coventry and North W while employed
at Daimlarm Coventry.

Brother, P.A. Meldon, played for MCC.

MELVILLE, James – RHB SLA
b. Barrow-in-Furness, Lancs., 15 March
1909; d. Coventry, 2 August 1961.
Educated at Barrow Grammar School.

Debut 1946 v Hants, Edgbaston. 2
matches for W 1946 (amateur). Highest

score: W 13 v Kent, Edgbaston 1946. Best
bowling: W 3–34 v Hants, on debut.

Played for Millom and Courtaulds.

Soccer   for   Blackburn   Rovers,
Northampton Town, Hull City.

MENCE, Michael David – LHB RM
b. Newbury, Berks., 13 April 1944.

Educated at Bradfield School.

Debut 1962 v Middx., Lord's. 31 matches for W 1962–65. Highest score: W 53 v Lancs., Coventry Courtaulds 1964. Best bowling: W 5–26 v Derby., Derby 1964.

22 matches for Glos., 1966–67; highest first-class score 78 v Sussex, Hove 1967. Full first-class record; 949 runs (15.06); 86 wickets (35.46). Played for Berks.: 1961; 1968–81. Appeared for Smethwick in Birmingham League.

Father, J.A. Mence, played for Berks.

d. Loughborough, Leics., 30 September 1957.

Debut v Kent, Edgbaston 1920. 2 matches for W 1920. Highest score: W 9 v Leics., Edgbaston 1920.

Played in Birmingham League for Aston Unity, Old Hill, Dudley, Stourbridge. Also played for Lincoln Lindum CC. Played for Lincs. in Minor Counties Championship.

Soccer, Everton and Lincoln City.

MERRICK, Tyrone Anthony – RHB RFM
b. St John's, Antigua, 10 June 1963. Educated at All Saints School, Antigua.

Debut 1987 v Surrey, Edgbaston 1987. 31 matches for W 1987–88 (cap 1988). Highest score: W 74* v Glos., Edgbaston 1987. Best bowling: W 7–45 (13–115 match) v Lancs., Edgbaston 1987. Achieved hat trick, 4 wickets in 5 balls and 6 wickets in 10 balls during spell of 6–29 v Derby., Derby 1988.

Played for Leeward Islands since 1982.

MEUNIER, James Brown – RHB RF
b. Poynton, Stockport, Cheshire, c 1885;

MILBURN, Edward Thomas – RHB RM
b. Nuneaton, 15 September 1967.

Educated at Bablake School, Coventry.
  Debut v Hants, Edgbaston 1987. 3
matches for W 1987. Highest score: W 24
on debut. Best bowling: 1–26 same match.

Mitchells & Butlers; also played for
Milnrow and Philadelphia.

MILLER, Harry Rayment – RHB RMF
b. Gravesend, Kent, 22 February 1907; d.
Inverness, Scotland, 1 September 1966.
Educated at Solihull Grammar School and
Birmingham U.
  Debut 1928 v Worcs., Edgbaston (only
match – amateur). Scored 8 only innings;
took 1–38 in only bowl.
  Captained Birmingham U 1928. Played
for Knowle & Dorridge.
  Second Master at Ardingly College for
several years until his death.

MILLS, John Michael – RHB LBG
b. Birmingham, 27 July 1921.
  Educated at Oundle and Corpus Christi
College, Cambridge.
  Debut 1946 v Essex, Edgbaston. 4
matches for W 1946 (amateur). Highest
score: W 26 v Glam., Edgbaston 1946.
Best bowling: W 2–67 same match.
  Cambridge U 1946–48 – Blue each
season, captain 1948. Highest first-class
score 44 Cambridge U v Essex, Cambridge
1947. Best first-class bowling 7–69

MILLER, Roland ('Ronnie') – RHB SLA
b. Philadelphia, Co. Durham, 6 January
1941.
  Debut 1961 v Cambridge U, Portland
Road. 133 matches for W 1961–68
(professional). Highest score: W 72 v
Worcs., Edgbaston 1965. Best bowling: W
6–28 v Lancs., Old Trafford 1963.
  Played in Birmingham League for Aston
Unity, West Bromwich Dartmouth,

Cambridge U v Yorks., Cambridge 1946.
Full first-class record: 743 runs (14.86); 95
wickets (28.87).

Son J.P.C. Mills played for Cambridge
U and Northants.

MITCHELL, Frank Rollason – RHB RM
b. Goulborn, Australia, 3 June 1922; d.
Myton Hamlet, Warwick, 4 April 1984.
Educated at John Gulson School,
Coventry.

Debut 1946 v Leics., Edgbaston. 17
matches for W 1946–48 (professional).
Highest score: W 43 v Worcs., Edgbaston
1946. Best bowling: W 4–69 v Leics.,
Edgbaston 1946.

Played for Cornwall 1951.

Professional coach at Dulwich,
groundsman/professional at Kynoch,
Aston Unity, Stourbridge (Birmingham
League), Knowle & Dorridge. Soccer for
Birmingham, Chelsea and Watford.

MOLES, Andrew James – RHB RM
b. Solihull, 12 February 1961. Educated at
Finham Park Comprehensive, Coventry
and Butts College of Higher Education,
Coventry.

Debut 1986 v Lancs., Old Trafford. 54
matches for W 1986–88 (cap 1987). Highest
score: W 151 v Kent, Edgbaston 1987. Best
bowling: W 3–21 v Oxford U, Oxford 1987.
1431 runs (33.27) 1987.

Played for Griqualand West since

1986–87. Highest first-class score 200* Griq
W v N. Transvaal 'B', Kimberley 1987–88.
Full first-class record: 4499 runs (41.65).
Played for Moseley in Birmingham
League.

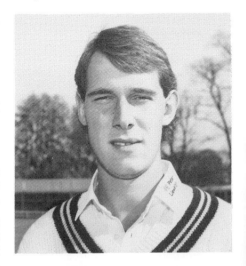

MONKHOUSE, Steven – RHB LFM
b. Bury, Lancs., 24 November 1962.

Educated at Derby Technical Grammar School and Peel College, Bury.

Debut 1985 v Surrey, The Oval. 2 matches for W 1985–86. Highest score: W 7 on debut. Best bowling: W 1–34 v Lancs., Edgbaston 1986.

Played for Glam. 1987–88.

Northampton 1926.

Played for Olton CC; also cricket in S. America 1920–24.

Director, Birmingham FC 1932–80.

MOORHOUSE, Fred – RHB RM
b. Berry Brow, Yorks., 25 March 1880; d. Dudley Guest Hospital, 7 April 1933.

Debut 1900 v London County, Crystal Palace. 117 matches: W 1900–08 (professional – capped). Highest score: W 75 v London Counties, Crystal Palace 1904. Best bowling: W 7–53 v Yorks., Hull 1903.

League professional in north of England; also played for Cheshire.

Brother, Robert Moorhouse, played for Yorks.

MORRIS, Leonard John – LHB RMF
b. Birmingham, 26 September 1898; d. Dorridge, Solihull, 9 March 1984. Educated at King Edward's, Camp Hill, Birmingham.

Debut 1925, v Worcs. at Dudley. 7 matches for W 1925–26 (amateur). Highest score: W 76 v Glam., Swansea 1926. Best bowling: W 2–41 v Northants,

MORTER, Frank William – RHB RMF
b. High Elms Gardens, Down, Kent, 14 August 1897; d. Birmingham Accident Hospital, 20 December 1958.

Debut 1922 v Yorks., Huddersfield. 3 matches for W 1922 (amateur). Highest score: W 8 on debut. Best bowling: W 2–5 v Leics., Leicester 1922.

Played for Moseley (Birmingham League).

MORTON, John – RHB
b. Drapers Field, Coventry, 17 August
1895; d. Leamington Spa, 28 May 1966.
Educated at King Henry VIII School,
Coventry.
   Debut 1929 v Surrey, Edgbaston. 9
matches for W 1929–30 (amateur). Highest
score: W 38 v Som., Edgbaston 1930. W
Committee 1950–54.
   Played for Coventry and North W.

MORTON, William – LHB SLA
b. Stirling, Scotland, 21 April 1961.
Educated at Wallace High School, Stirling.

   Debut 1984 v Surrey, Edgbaston. 10
matches for W 1984–85. Highest score: W
13* on debut. Best bowling: W 4–85 v
Glam., Edgbaston 1984.
   Played for Scotland 1982–83.
   Club: Stirling County.

MUNTON, Timothy Alan – RHB RFM
b. Melton Mowbray, Leics., 30 July 1965.
Educated at Sarson High School; King
Edward VII Upper School.
   Debut 1985 v Zimbabweans, Edgbaston.
51 matches for W 1985–date. Highest
score: W 38 v Yorks., Scarborough 1987.
Best bowling: W 6–21 v Worcs., Edgbaston
1988.

MURRAY, Athol Leslie – RHB RMF
b. Mill Hill, Middx., 29 June 1901; d.
Grasmere, Westmorland, 10 January 1981.
Educated at St George's, Harpenden and
Oxford U.
   Debut 1922 v Surrey, Edgbaston. 11
matches for W 1922 (amateur). Highest
score: W 33 on debut. Best bowling: W
2–29 v Hants, Southampton 1922.

Educated at Queen's College, Port-of-Spain, Jesus College, Cambridge and Nottingham U.

Debut 1972 v Middx., Edgbaston. 58 matches for W 1972–75 (cap 1972). Highest score: W 78 v Glam., Edgbaston 1974.

Played for Trinidad 1960–61 to 1980–81; Cambridge Blue 1965–66 (captain 1966); 97 matches for Notts. 1966–69 (cap 1967); 62 Tests for W. Indies 1963–80 (captain once). Test record: 1993 runs (22–90); 181 catches, 8 stumpings. Full first-class record: 13289 runs (28.33); 741 catches, 108 stumpings. Highest first-class score 166* Notts. v Surrey, The Oval 1966.

His father, Lance Murray, played for Trinidad; and cousin, Colin Murray, played for Trinidad and Warwickshire II.

Played club cricket for Knowle & Dorridge, Rowington. W Committee 1935–45.

Captained Oxford U at golf 1922–23.

MYLES, Simon David – RHB RM
b. Mansfield, Notts, 2 June 1966. Educated at King George V School, Hong Kong.

Debut 1988 v Leics., Edgbaston 1988. 3 matches for W 1988. Highest score: 39 on debut.

Played twice for Sussex 1987; Represented Hong Kong in 1986 ICC Trophy, scoring 172 v Gibraltar at Bridgnorth.

MURRAY, Deryck Lance – RHB WK LB
b. Port-of-Spain, Trinidad, 20 May 1943.

N

NELSON, Alfred Leonard – RHB occ. WK
b. Crackley Hill, Kenilworth, 13
November 1871; d. Holly Green, Worcs., 2
May 1927. Educated at Radley and Merton
College, Oxford.

Debut 1895 v Lancs., Liverpool (only
match – amateur). Dismissed for 0 in each
innings.

Played club cricket for Leamington and
Kenilworth.

Nephew, G.M.B. Nelson, played for W.

NELSON, Guy Montague Blyth – RHB
RFM
b. Coten End, Warwick, 28 August 1900;
d. Great Bourton, near Banbury, Oxon.,
13 January 1969. Educated at Rugby and
Trinity College, Cambridge.

Debut 1921 v Worcs., Worcester. 13
matches for W 1921–22 (amateur). Highest
score: W 21 v Cambridge U, Edgbaston
1921. Best bowling: W 4–53 v Surrey,
Edgbaston 1921.

Played for Leamington and Kenilworth
clubs.

Uncle, A.L. Nelson, played for W.

NORTON, Ernest Willmott – RHB LBG
b. Sparkhill, Birmingham; 19 June 1889; d.
Birmingham, April 1972. Educated at King
Edward's, Camp Hill, Birmingham.

Debut 1920 v Leics., Edgbaston. 2
matches for W 1920 (amateur). Highest
score: W 26* on debut.

Also played 6 times for Worcs. 1922–23.
Club cricket for Harborne, Knowle
Dorridge and King's Heath.

OAKES, Dennis Raymond – RHB LB
b. Bedworth, 10 April 1946. Educated at Nicholas Chamberlain Comprehensive, Bedworth.

Debut 1965 v Northants, Peterborough. 5 matches for W 1965. Highest score: W 33 v Worcs., Worcester 1965.

Played for Bedworth CC.

Runs schoolboy coaching for County Club and NCA in Nuneaton, Bedworth and Coventry. Played soccer for Coventry City, Notts County and Peterborough.

OLD, Alan Gerald Bernard – RHB RMF
b. Middlesbrough, Yorks., 23 September

1945. Educated at Acklam Hall Grammar School, Middlesbrough.

Debut 1969 v Cambridge U, Edgbaston (only match) Highest score: 34.

Played for Durham 1968–78; clubs include Middlesbrough, Sheffield Collegiate.

Rugby Union for Middlesbrough, Leicester and Sheffield; 16 caps for England and toured S. Africa with British Lions 1974.

Brother, C.M. Old, played for Yorks and W.

OLD, Christopher Middleton ('Chilly') – LHB RFM
b. Middlesbrough, Yorks. 22 December 1948. Educated at Acklam Hall Grammar School, Middlesbrough.

Debut 1983 v Northants, Edgbaston. 47 matches for W 1983–85 (cap 1984). Highest score: W 70 v Worcs., Edgbaston 1984.

Best bowling: W 6–46 v Yorks., Leeds 1984.

Played 222 matches for Yorks. 1966–82; capped 1969, benefit 1979; captain 1981. Highest first-class score 116 Yorks. v India, Bradford 1974. Best first-class bowling 7–20 Yorks. v Glos., Middlesbrough 1969. 46 Tests for England 1972–73 to 1981: best Test bowling 7–50 v Pakistan, Edgbaston 1978, at one time taking 4 wickets in 5 balls. Test record: 845 runs (14.82); 143 wickets (28.11). Full first-class record: 7756 runs (20.30) 6 centuries; 1070 wickets (23.44). Played for Northumberland 1986–87.

Club: Middlesbrough. Career strewn with injuries throughout. Brother, Alan Old, played for W.

OLIVER, Philip Robert – RHB RM OB
b. West Bromwich, Staffs., 9 May 1956. Educated at Newport Secondary Modern School, Salop.

Debut 1975 v Glam., Swansea. 82 matches for W 1975–82. Highest score: W 171* v Northants, Northampton 1981. Best bowling: W 2–28 v Sussex, Edgbaston 1978.

Played for Salop 1972–74; 1986; Staffs. 1987–date. Old Hill (Birmingham League), Newport, Penn.

Hip replacement operation 1986; returned to top 1988 Minor Counties batting averages.

ORD, James Simpson – RHB
b. Backworth, Northumberland, 12 July 1912.

Debut 1933 v Essex, Leyton. 273 matches for W 1933–53 (professional – cap 1935). Benefit (£4,934) 1950.

Highest score: W 187* v Cambridge U, Cambridge 1952. 1000 runs (6); 1577 (39.42) 1948 best. Scored 107* and 101 in match, v Notts., Trent Bridge 1948. Added 250 with H.E. Dollery v Kent, Maidstone 1953; County 7th wicket record.

Played for Aston Unity in Birmingham League.

Brother, J.D. Ord, played for Northumberland.

O'ROURKE, Christopher – RHB WK
b. Widnes, Lancs., 13 March 1945.

Debut 1968 v Scotland, Edgbaston (only match). 23* only innings.

P

PAINE, George Alfred Edward – RHB SLA

b. Paddington, London, 11 June 1908; d. Solihull, 30 March 1978. Educated at Droop Street School, Paddington.

Debut 1929 v Glos., Edgbaston. 240 matches for W 1929–47 (professional – cap 1929). Benefit (£881) 1938. Highest score: W 79 v Glam., Edgbaston 1933. Best bowling: W 8–43 (12–89 match) v Worcs., Edgbaston 1934. 100 wickets (5); 155 (16.94) 1934 best. Hat tricks: v Middx., Lord's 1932, v Glamorgan, Cardiff 1933.

Played 5 matches for Middx. 1926. 4 Tests for England, v West Indies 1934–35: 5–168 v W. Indies, Kingston 1934–35. Test record 97 runs (16.16); 17 wickets (27.47). Full first-class record: 3430 runs (11.95); 1021 wickets (22.85). Played in Birmingham League for Mitchells & Butlers, Kidderminster, Moseley, Smethwick, Walsall.

Professional coach/groundsman Solihull School to 1969.

PALLETT, Henry James ('Knack') – RHB OB or LB

b. Birchfields, Birmingham, 2 January 1863; d. Aston, Birmingham, 18 June 1917. Educated at Trinity School, Birchfields.

Debut 1894 v Notts., Trent Bridge (played non-first-class from 1883). 73 matches for W 1894–98 (professional – capped). Benefit (£500) 1897. Highest score: W 55* v Surrey, The Oval 1896. Best bowling: W 9–55 v Essex, Leyton 1894.

First-class debut England XI v Australia, Edgbaston 1886. Played for Aston Unity, Stourbridge, Smethwick, West Bromwich, Dartmouth.

PALMER, George Arthur – RHB RFM
b. Hopsford Hale, Withybrook, W 5 June

137

G.A.E. Paine played 240 matches for Warwickshire and took 1021 wickets in his career

1897; d. Higham-on-the-Hill, Leics., 1 June 1962.

Debut 1928 v Glam., Edgbaston. 9 matches for W 1928 (amateur). Highest score: W 20 on debut. Best bowling: W 2–21 on debut.

Club cricket for Hinckley.

PARKES, Howard Roderick – RHB
b. Erdington, Birmingham, 31 May 1877;

d. Studland, Dorset, 28 May 1920 (death from effects of wartime mustard-gas poisoning). Educated at Uppingham and Christ Church College, Oxford.

Debut 1898 v Leics., Leicester (only match – amateur). Scored 1 in only innings.

Played 6 matches for London County 1900, and played for Moseley (Birmingham League).

PARRY, Matthew Croose – RHB RM
b. Birley, Herefordshire, 12 December 1885; d. Carrigrohane, Co. Cork, Ireland, 5 February 1931. Educated at Hereford Cathedral School and Birmingham U.

Debut 1908 v Lancs., Edgbaston. 2 matches for W 1908–10 (amateur). Highest score: W 10, on debut and v Northants, Edgbaston 1910.

Played for Ireland 1925, scoring 124 v Scotland, Dublin. Bowling figures 2–31, Ireland v Wales, Llandudno 1925.

PARSONS, Gordon James – LHB RMF
b. Slough, Bucks., 17 October 1959. Educated at Woodside County School, Slough.

Debut 1986 v Essex, Edgbaston. 47 matches for W 1986–88 (cap 1987). Highest score: W 67* v Notts., Edgbaston 1987. Best bowling: W 7–16 v Cambridge U, Cambridge 1988.

Played 118 matches for Leics. 1978–85 (cap 1984). Returned there for 1989. Played for Boland (1983–84 to 1984–85) and Griqualand West (1985–86 to 1986–87) Highest first-class score: 76 Boland v W. Province B, Cape Town 1984–85. Best first-class bowling: 9–72 Boland v Transvaal B, Jo'burg 1984–85. Full first-class record: 3647 runs (19.19); 444 wickets (30.33).

PARSONS, (Canon) John Henry – RHB RM
b. Oxford, 30 May 1890; d. Plymouth, Devon, 2 February 1981. Educated at Bablake School, Coventry.

Debut 1910 v Derby., Edgbaston. 313 matches for Warwickshire 1910–34 (professional 1910–14; 1924–28; amateur 1919–23; 1929–34 – capped c 1911). Benefit (£881) 1926. Highest score: W 225 v Glam., Edgbaston 1927. Best bowling: W 4–13 v Lancs., Old Trafford 1925. 1000 runs (8), 1671 (50.63) in 1927 best.

Played for Europeans in India 1919–20 to 1921–22; figures of 7–41 (13–115 match) at Madras 1919–20. Tour, MCC to India 1926–27 – scored 1289 runs (49.57). Full first-class record: 17969 runs (35.72); 38 centuries; 83 wickets (28.97).

Ordained Church of England deacon 1929, priest in 1930; the only professional cricketer to become a parson.

PARTRIDGE, Norman Ernest – RHB RMF
b. Great Barr, Staffs., 10 August 1900; d. Aberystwyth, Wales, 10 March 1982. Educated at Malvern and Pembroke College, Cambridge.

Debut 1921 v Cambridge U, Cambridge. 100 matches for W 1921–37 (amateur – capped). Highest score: W 102 v Som., Edgbaston 1925. Best bowling: W 7–66 v Derby., Edgbaston 1923. W Committee 1930–47.

Won Cambridge Blue 1920. Full first-class record: 2719 runs (18.62); 393 wickets (23.02). Invited to play for Gentlemen v Players, The Oval 1919 while still at school; headmaster refused permission! Played for Walsall and West Bromwich Dartmouth in Birmingham League, Wolverhampton and Hampton-in-Arden.

PAUL, Nigel Aldridge – RHB LFM
b. Surbiton, Surrey, 31 March 1933.

Educated at Cranleigh.

Debut 1954 v Canada, Edgbaston. 4 matches for W 1954–55 (amateur). Highest score: W 40 v Services, Edgbaston 1955.

Free Foresters 1956, D.R. Jardine's XI 1958. Clubs: Esher (Surrey), Harborne.

PEARE, William George – RHB RMF
b. Waterford, Ireland, 25 July 1905; d. St Luke's Co. Cork, 16 November 1979. Educated at Morgan's School, Castleknock, Dublin.

Debut 1926 v Hants, Edgbaston. 7 matches for W 1926 (professional). Highest score: W 12* v Yorks., Edgbaston 1926. Best bowling: W 1–4 v Worcs., Edgbaston 1926.

Played for MCC v Ireland, Rathmines 1936, having innings bowling analysis 3–45. Played for Aston Unity in Birmingham League.

Became President, Cork CCC.

PELL, Godfrey Arnold – RHB LBG
b. Sunderland, Co. Durham, 11 March 1928. Educated at King Edward's, Edgbaston.

Debut 1947 v Scotland, Edgbaston (only match – amateur). Highest score: W 16*. Best bowling: W 2–9.

Played for Moseley in Birmingham League.

PEREIRA, Edward Thomas – RHB
b. Wolseley Hall, Colwich, Staffs., 26 September 1866; d. Edgbaston, 25 February 1939. Educated at the Oratory School, Birmingham.

Debut 1895 v Kent, Canterbury (non-first-class in 1886). 5 matches for W

1895–96 (amateur). Highest score: 34 on debut.

Played 2 matches for MCC 1900. Played in Birmingham League for Dudley.

A Catholic priest, the first to play for the County, he became Head of the Oratory School, remaining there until his death.

PERKINS, Hubert George – LHB SLA
b. Attleborough, Nuneaton, 18 June 1907; d. Nuneaton, 4 May 1935. Educated at Attleborough School.

Debut 1926 v Glam., Edgbaston. 4 matches for W. 1926–27 (professional). Highest score: W 6* v Glam., Edgbaston 1926. Best bowling: W 1–30 on debut.

Appeared for Attleborough CC.

PERRYMAN, Stephen Peter – RHB RM
b. Yardley, Birmingham, 22 October 1955.

Educated   at   Sheldon   Heath Comprehensive.

Debut 1974 v Cambridge U, Nuneaton Griff & Coton. 131 matches for W 1974–81 (cap 1977). Highest score: W 43 v Som., Edgbaston 1977. Best bowling: W 7–49 v Hants, Bournemouth 1978.

25 matches for Worcs. 1982–83. Full first-class record: 872 runs (9.27); 358 wickets (31.66). An indifferent batsman – failed to score in first 8 innings for Worcs. 1982. Played for Mitchells & Butlers (Birmingham League), and for Staffs. in Minor Counties 1988.

Coaching   assistant   at   Warwickshire Indoor School.

PHILLIPS, Hugh Raymond – RHB
b. Kuala Lumpur, Malaya, 8 April 1929. Educated at Wellingborough.

Debut 1951 v Scotland (only match – amateur). Highest score: W 3.

Represented   Malaya   in   Asian Competition. Played for King's Heath.

PHILLIPS, Joseph Herbert – RHB RFM
b. Ansley, W 2 December 1881; d. Oldbury   Grange,   Atherstone,   after domestic accident, 15 January 1951.

Debut 1904 v London County, Coventry and North W. 6 matches for W 1904–11 (amateur; captain on 4 occasions). Highest score: W 16 v Lancs., Edgbaston 1910. Best bowling: W 1–30 v Derby., Blackwell Colliery 1910.

Clubs included Ansley Hall, Nuneaton, Coleshill.

Rugby Union, Nuneaton and Midland Counties. Grandfather of Capt. Mark Phillips, husband of HRH, The Princess Royal.

PIERSON, Adrian Roger Kirshaw – RHB OB
b. Enfield, Middx. 21 July 1963. Educated at Kent College, Canterbury; Hatfield Polytechnic.

Debut 1985 v Oxford U, Oxford. 25 matches for W 1985–date. Highest score: W 42* v Northants, Northampton 1986. Best bowling: W 3–33 v Worcs., Edgbaston 1988.

POTTER, Wilfred – RHB LB
b. Swincliffe Top, Felliscliffe, Yorks. 2 May 1910.

Debut 1932 v Derby., Derby (only match – professional). Failed to score either innings. Best bowling: W 1–19.

Played for Sparkhill Belvedere, Harborne Somerville and Birmingham City Transport.

Was assistant groundsman at Edgbaston, working for his uncle, Ted Leyland. Maurice Leyland (Yorks. and England) was his cousin.

PRIDMORE, Reginald George – RHB
b. Edgbaston, 29 April 1886; d. in action, Piave River, north of Venice, Italy, 13 March 1918. Educated at Elstow School, Bedford.

Debut 1909 v Yorks., Edgbaston. 14 matches for W 1909–12 (amateur). Highest score: W 49 v Derby., Coventry and North W 1909.

Fine hockey player; played for Herts. and represented England in 1908 Olympics.

PRITCHARD, Thomas Leslie – RHB RF/FM
b. Kaupokonui, New Zealand, 10 March 1917. Educated at Hawera Technical High School.

Debut 1946 v India, Edgbaston. 170 matches for W 1946–55 (professional – cap 1947). Benefit (£3,816) 1952. Highest

A good-humoured group of Warwickshire players from the early 1950s. Left to right: Eric Hollies, Ray Hitchcock, Alan Townsend (and daughter), Ray Weeks and Tom Pritchard

score: W 81 v Notts., Edgbaston 1947. Best bowling: W 8–20 v Worcs., Dudley 1950. 100 wickets (3); 166 (17.94) 1948 best. Three hat tricks for W, v Leics., Edgbaston 1948; v Kent, Maidstone 1949; v Glam., Edgbaston 1951. 14–93 in match v Glamorgan, Edgbaston 1951.

Played for Wellington (N. Zealand) 1937–38 to 1940–41; toured England with New Zealand Services Team 1945. Appeared 4 times for Kent 1956, as amateur. Full first-class record 3363 runs (13.34); 818 wickets (23.30). Played in Birmingham League for Moseley, Smethwick, West Bromwich Dartmouth and Stourbridge.

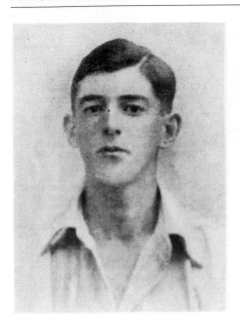

PUGH, John Geoffrey – RHB RM
b. Radford, Coventry, 22 January 1904; d. Hastings, Barbados, 12 February 1964. Educated at Rugby School.

Debut 1922 v Northants, Edgbaston. 9 matches for W 1922–27 (amateur). Highest score: W 41 v Surrey, The Oval 1922. Best bowling: W 4–100 v Worcs., Worcester 1927.

Club cricket for Rugby. Nephew, C.T.M. Pugh, played for Glos.

QUAIFE, Bernard William – RHB WK RA bowler
b. Olton, Solihull, 24 November 1899; d. Bridport, Dorset, 27 November 1984. Educated at Solihull Grammar School.

Debut 1920 v Som., Bath. 48 matches for W 1920–26 (amateur – capped). Highest score: W 99* v Northants, Edgbaston 1923. Best bowling: W 1–4 v Leics., Edgbaston 1923. 271 matches for Worcs. 1928–37. Highest first-class score: 136* Worcs. v Leics., Worcester 1928. Best first-class bowling 2–5 Worcs. v Leics., Leicester 1934. 9594 runs (20.02); 186 caught, 54 stumped in first-class career.

Played for Olton CC. Father, W.G. Quaife, played for W; uncle, Walter Quaife, played for Sussex and W.

QUAIFE, Walter – RHB RM
b. Newhaven, Sussex, 1 March 1864; d. Norwood, Surrey, 18 January 1943.

Debut 1894 v Notts., Trent Bridge (non-first-class games in 1893). 121 matches for W 1894–1901 (professional – capped in 1894). Highest score: W 144 v Glos., Edgbaston 1899. Best bowling: W 2–5 v Lancs., Old Trafford 1897. 1161 runs (35.18) in 1895. Played 90 matches for Sussex 1884–91. Highest first-class score 156* Sussex v Glos., Hove 1890. Best first-class bowling 4–35 Sussex v Yorks., Hove 1886. First-class record; 8536 runs (22.88); 10 centuries. Played Handsworth Wood and Moseley in Birmingham League, and Suffolk (Minor Counties) Brother, W.G. Quaife, played for W; nephew, B.W. Quaife, played for W and Worcs.

QUAIFE, William (known as 'WG') – RHB RMF/LB
b. Newhaven, Sussex, 17 March 1872; d. Edgbaston, 13 October 1951.

Debut 1894 v Notts., Trent Bridge. (Played non-first-class 1893.) 665 matches for W 1894–1928 (professional – capped). Benefits (£410) 1910; (£917) 1928. Highest score: W 255* v Surrey, The Oval 1905 (then record score for Warwickshire; still record second innings score and best for a no. 4 in batting order). Best bowling: W

147

7–76 (12–127 match) v Worcs., Edgbaston 1901. 1000 runs (20 – county record equalled by Amiss in 1987); 1933 (60.40) 1905 best. Holds W partnership records for 3rd wicket – 327 with S Kinneir v Lancs., Edgbaston 1901, and 5th wicket – 268 with Walter Quaife v Essex, Leyton 1900. Record of 71 centuries for W beaten by Dennis Amiss 1985. Scored 124 and 109 v Surrey, The Oval 1913. 107 next innings, v Northants, Edgbaston. Carried bat through innings – 178 out of 475 – v Hants, Southampton 1897. Scored final century – 115 v Derby., Edgbaston 1928 – aged 56 years, 140 days; oldest century-maker in County Championship.

7 Tests for England 1899 to 1901–02; 228 runs (19.00). Played for Griqualand West 1912–13. Full first-class record: 36012 runs (35.37); 72 centuries; 931 wickets (27.32). Played for Mitchells & Butlers, Moseley, West Bromwich Dartmouth and Handsworth Wood in Birmingham League; also Olton CC.

Son, B.W. Quaife, played for W and Worcs., brother, Walter Quaife, played for Sussex and W.

*The great W.G. Quaife who, at 33862 runs in his first-class career, was
Warwickshire's highest-scoring batsman until Dennis Amiss superseded him*

RATCLIFFE, David Philip – RHB
b. Hall Green, Birmingham, 11 May 1939.

Debut 1957 v Scotland, Edgbaston. 20 matches for W 1957–68 (professional). Highest score: W 79 v Scotland, Edgbaston 1961.

Played for Mitchells & Butlers, Moseley, West Bromwich Dartmouth in Birmingham League; also Pickwick CC.

Son, Jason Ratcliffe, plays for W.

RATCLIFFE, Jason David – RHB
b. Solihull, 19 June 1969. Educated at Sharman's Cross School, Solihull.

Debut 1988 v Sussex, Hove. 2 matches for W 1988. Highest score: 16 on debut.

Attached to Moseley CC. Father, David Ratcliffe, played for W.

REEVE, Dermot Alexander – RHB RMF
b. Kowloon, Hong Kong, 2 April 1963. Educated at King George V School, Kowloon.

Debut 1988 v Lancs., Old Trafford. 16 matches for W 1988. Highest score. W 103 v Northants, Northampton 1988. Best bowling: W 4–50 v Yorks., Edgbaston 1988.

Played for Sussex 1983–87 (cap 1986). Highest first-class score 119 Sussex v

Surrey, Guildford 1984. Best first-class bowling 7–37 Sussex v Lancs., Lytham 1987. First-class record: 2192 runs (24.35); 263 wickets (28.43). Played for Hong Kong 1980–83.

RHODES, James – RHB
b. Aston, Birmingham, 27 July 1866; d. Solihull, 26 August 1939. Educated at Mason's College, Birmingham; Saltley College, Birmingham.

Debut 1895 v Derby., Edgbaston. 3 matches for W 1895 (amateur). Highest score: W 64 on debut.

Played for Aston Unity in Birmingham League.

RHODES, Thomas Basil – RHB occ. WK
b. Uttoxeter, Staffs., 13 August 1874; d. Worthing, Sussex, 26 May 1936. Educated at Malvern.

Debut 1899 v Glos., Bristol. 4 matches for W 1899 (amateur). Highest score: W 55 on debut.

Played for Worcs. in pre-first-class days (1894–95–96).

Club: Wolverhampton.

RICE, William Ignatius – RHB RM
b. Birmingham, 15 March 1883; d. Douai

Abbey School, Woolhampton, Berks. 22
April 1955. Educated at Douai Abbey.
   Debut 1920 v Oxford U, Oxford. 2
matches for W 1920 (amateur). Highest
score: 9 on debut.
   Played for Knowle & Dorridge 1903–30.
   As Revd Father Ignatius, Member of the
Order of St Benedict, was the first monk to
play first-class cricket.

Brothers Peter (Kent. Worcs. and
England) and Dick (Worcs. and England)
Richardson.

RICHARDS, Walter – RHB OB
b. Balsall Heath, Birmingham, 28
September 1865; d. Hollywood, near
Birmingham, 14 October 1917.
   Debut 1895 v Essex, Leyton (played
non-first-class from 1883). 7 matches for W
1895–96 (professional – capped). Joint-
benefit (£100 each) with S.J. Whitehead
1904. Highest score: W 61* v Lancs.,
Edgbaston 1895.
   Played for Salter's and West Bromwich
Dartmouth, Birmingham League, also
Pickwick CC. Coached in Cape Town
1899–1900.
   First-class umpire 1898–1914.

RICHARDSON, Bryan Anthony – LHB
RALB
b. Kenilworth, 24 February 1944.
Educated at Malvern.
   Debut 1963 v Scotland, Edinburgh. 40
matches for W 1963–67. Highest score: W
126 v Cambridge U, Edgbaston 1967
(scored 105 in second innings).
   Played for Smethwick (Birmingham
League).

RICHARDSON, Stanley Hugh – RHB
b. Marston Green, 2 July 1890; d.
Cambridge, 24 January 1958.
   Debut 1920 v Kent, Catford. 2 matches
for W 1920 (amateur). Highest score: W 8*
v Kent, Edgbaston 1920. Played 1 game for
Notts. 1925. Appeared for Aston Unity
(Birmingham League) and Yardley;
subsequently Notts Amateurs.

RILEY, Terence Michael Noel ('Terry') –
RHB occ. LB

b. Birmingham, 25 December 1939. Educated at Wellesbourne School, Birmingham.

Debut 1961 v Derby., Derby. 12 matches for W 1961–64 (professional). Highest score: W 84 on debut.

11 matches for Glos. 1964. Played for Aston Unity (Birmingham League), Knowle & Dorridge, Pickwick, Old Silhillians.

Debut 1949 v Cambridge U, Cambridge. 5 matches for W 1949–50 (professional). Highest score: W 30 on debut.

Played in Coventry League for GEC and Courtaulds; also Coventry and North W.

ROBERTS, Harley James – RHB RM
b. Bearwood, Staffs., 24 May 1912; d. Romsley, Worcs., 17 February 1989. Educated at Bourne College, Quinton.

Debut 1932 v Middx., Edgbaston. 17 matches for W 1932–37 (professional, amateur from 1935). Highest score: W 61 v Essex, Chelmsford 1932. Best bowling: W 3–6 on debut (took 2 wickets in first over in first-class cricket).

Played for Mitchells & Butlers (Birmingham League) and Harborne.

Top-class amateur golfer. Father played as professional for Staffs. 1892.

ROBERTS, Harry Edmund – LHB RM
b. Earlsdon, Coventry, 5 June 1924. Educated at Bablake School, Coventry.

ROBINS, Derrick Harold – RHB WK
b. Bexley Heath, Kent, 27 June 1914. Educated at Champion Hill House,

Dulwich.

Debut 1947 v Middx., Edgbaston. 2 matches for W 1947 (amateur). Highest score: W 29* on debut.

Played 3 first-class matches for D.H. Robins' XI 1969–71; organiser of this team which played against touring and university teams, and undertook tours (usually S. Africa). Played for Coventry and North W and Leamington.

Former Chairman, Coventry City FC.

ROBINSON, Maurice – RHB RM
b. Lisburn, N. Ireland, 17 July 1921.

Debut 1951 v Scotland, Edgbaston. 8 matches for W 1951–52 (amateur). Highest score W 57 v Services, Edgbaston 1951.

66 matches for Glam. 1946–50 (cap 1950). Played for European teams, Hyderabad and Madras in India, 1942–45. Highest first-class score: 190 Glam. v Hants, Bournemouth 1949. Best first-class bowling: 7–51 Madras Europeans v India 1944–45. Full first-class record: 2719 runs (22.10); 2 centuries; 34 wickets (25.58). Appeared for Moseley in Birmingham League.

ROBINSON, Thomas Lloyd – RHB RMF
b. Swansea, S. Wales, 21 December 1912. Educated at Wycliffe College.

Debut 1946 v Derby., Edgbaston. 4 matches for W 1946. Highest score: W 13* v India, Edgbaston 1946. Best bowling: W 2–74 Essex, Southend 1946.

Played for Moseley Ashfield and Clifton. Rugby Union for Moseley and North

Midlands.

Wife's uncle was F.R. Foster (W and England).

ROLL, Henry – RHB RM
b. Alloa, Scotland, 18 March 1905; d. Downend, Glos., 25 May 1967.

Debut 1927 v New Zealand, Edgbaston (only match – professional). 0 in only innings; 0 wickets.

Club cricket for Feltham CC and Ashford (Middlesex) CC. Grandson, L.H. Roll, played for Glos.

ROTHERHAM, Gerard Alexander ('Gerry') – RHB RM

b. Allesley, Coventry, 28 May 1899; d. Bakewell, Derby., 31 January 1985. Educated at Rugby School and Trinity College, Cambridge.

Debut 1919 v Northants, Edgbaston, 44 matches for W 1919–21 (amateur). Highest score: W 62 v Leics., Hinckley 1920. Best bowling: W 7–69 v Glos., Clifton 1921.

Played for Cambridge U 1919–20 (Blue 1919). Assisted Wellington (New Zealand) 1928–29. Highest first-class score 84* Cambridge U v Australian Forces, Cambridge 1919. Played for Moseley (Birmingham League) and Coventry and North Warwicks.

Uncle, Hugh Rotherham, played for W.

ROTHERHAM, Hugh – RHB RF WK
b. Allesley, Coventry, 16 March 1861; d. Coventry, 24 February 1939. Educated at Uppingham.

Debut 1903 v Philadelphians, Coventry and North Warwickshire. 1 match for W 1903 (non-first-class debut 1883 – captain – amateur). Highest score: W 33 in only innings.

First-class cricket for various Gentlemen's teams from 1880 – debut England team v Cambridge U, Cambridge 1880. Best first-class bowling 8–57 (14–150 match) Gentlemen v Oxford U, Oxford 1884. Full first-class record: 179 runs (7.16); 101 wickets (19.84). Toured N. America with E.J. Sanders' XI 1886.

Formerly fast bowler – 1903 appearance as wicketkeeper. Played for Coventry and North W.

Played rugby football for Coventry; captain, Coventry Golf Club. Nephew, G.A. Rotherham, played for W.

ROUSE, Stephen John – LHB LFM
b. Merthyr Tydfil, S. Wales, 20 January 1949. Educated at Moseley School, Birmingham.

Debut 1970 v Oxford U, Oxford. 120 matches for W 1970–81 (cap 1974). Highest score: W 93 v Hants, Bournemouth 1976. Best bowling: W 6–34 v Leics., Leicester 1976. Youth Coach, WCCC.

Groundsman, and former player, for Moseley (Birmingham League). Injuries hindered play.

RUSSELL, John Bernard – RHB WK
b. Rushall, Walsall, Staffs., 2 October 1883; d. Lichfield, Staffs., 18 August 1965. Educated at Bromsgrove School.

Debut 1920 v Cambridge U, Edgbaston (only match – amateur). Highest score: W 23.

Appeared for Staffs. and Sutton Coldfield CC.

S

SALE, Richard – LHB
b. Shrewsbury, 4 October 1919; d. Beccles, Suffolk, 3 February 1987. Educated at Repton and Oriel College, Oxford.
　Debut 1939 v Middx., Edgbaston. 19 matches for W 1939–47 (amateur – cap 1946). Highest score: W 157 v India, Edgbaston 1946. Played for Derby. 1949–54 (cap 1951). Played for Oxford U 1939, 1946 (Blue each season).
　Soccer Blue for Oxford. Father, R. Sale, played for Derby. Grandfather, R. Sale, on W Committee 1884–90.

SAM, Charles Alpheus ('Alphie') – LHB RM
b. St Vincent, 7 May 1953. Educated at Emmanuel High School, St Vincent.
　Two Sunday League matches 1979. Highest Score: W 31 v Yorks., Edgbaston on debut.
　Played for Leamington CC.

SANDERS, Wilfred ('Wib') – RHB RM
b. Chilvers Coton, Nuneaton, 4 April 1910; d. Nuneaton, 22 May 1965. Educated at Heath End Road School, Chilvers Coton.
　Debut 1928 v Yorks., Edgbaston. 84 matches for W 1928–34 (professional – cap 1930). Highest score: W 64 v Notts., Edgbaston 1930 (adding 126 for 9th wicket with F.R. Santall). Best bowling: W 4–44 v Northants, Coventry (Morris Motors) 1928. Added 128 with F.R. Santall v Yorks., Edgbaston 1930; still W 10th wicket record.

Played for Griff Colliery and Chilvers Coton and Smethwick in Birmingham League.

SANDERSON, Gerald Barry – RHB
b. Toxteth Park, Liverpool, 12 May 1881; d. Westminster, London, 3 October 1964. Educated at Malvern.
Debut 1901 v London County, Crystal Palace (only match – amateur). Run out 0 only innings.
Played 1 match for Worcs. 1923; run out 16 only innings. Played for Coventry and North W.

SANTALL, Frederick Reginald – RHB RM
b. Acocks Green, Birmingham, 12 July 1903; d. Cheltenham, Glos., 3 November 1950. Educated at Central Secondary School, Birmingham.
Debut 1919 v Worcs., Edgbaston aged 16 years, 23 days (W's youngest player). 496 matches for W 1919–39 (amateur until 1923, then professional – capped *c* 1924). Benefit (£712) 1935. Highest score: W 201* v Northants, Northampton 1933 (scored 173* before lunch, day 3). Best bowling: W 5–47 v Leics., Edgbaston 1936. 1000 runs (7): 1635 (45.41) 1933 best. 128 runs added

with W. Sanders v Yorks. at Edgbaston still county 10th wicket record.
Appeared for Moseley (Birmingham League) and King's Heath. Subsequently coached at Wrekin College, the Oratory School and Dean Close School, Cheltenham.
Father, S. Santall, played for W; brother, J.F.E. Santall, played for Worcs.

SANTALL, Sydney – RHB RM/OB
b. Peterborough, Northants, 10 June 1873;

d. Ensbury Park, Bournemouth, 19 March 1957. Educated at King's School, Peterborough.

Debut 1894 v Surrey, The Oval. 370 matches for W 1894–1914 (professional – capped). Benefit (£400) 1908. Highest score: W 73 v Derby., Edgbaston 1901. Best bowling: W 8–23 v Leics., Edgbaston 1900. 101 wickets (16.62) 1907. W coach 1920–37.

Played for West Bromwich Dartmouth and Mitchells & Butlers in Birmingham League. Appeared for Northants 1891.

Author: *History of Warwickshire Cricket* (1911); *Ten Years of First-class Cricket 1894–1903* (1904). Son, F.R. Santall, played for W; son, J.F.E. Santall, played for Worcs.

SAVAGE, Richard LeQuesne – RHB RM OB

b. Waterloo, London, 10 December 1955. Educated at Marlborough College and Pembroke College, Oxford.

Debut 1976 v Northants, Edgbaston 1976. 23 matches for W 1976–79. Highest score: W 15* v Som., Taunton 1979. Best bowling: W 7–50 v Glam., Nuneaton Griff & Coton 1977.

Played for Oxford U 1976–78 – Blue each season. Full first-class record: 127 wickets (29.81).

SCORER, Reginald Ivor ('Rusty') – RHB RFM

b. Middlesbrough, Yorks., 6 January 1892; d. Solihull, 19 March 1976. Educated at King Edward's School, Five Ways, Birmingham.

Debut 1921 v Surrey, Edgbaston. 29 matches for W 1921–26 (amateur). Highest score: W 113 v Northants, Edgbaston 1921. Best bowling: W 3–1 v Som., Taunton 1921.

Played for Handsworth Wood and Moseley in Birmingham League.

Organised wartime cricket festivals at Edgbaston (1941–45). Rugby football for Moseley; member RFU Committee 1947–72.

SHARP, Norman – RHB

b. Derby, 15 April 1901; d. Sutton

Coldfield, 14 July 1977. Educated at Bishop Vesey's Grammar School, Sutton Coldfield.

Debut 1923 v Worcs., Edgbaston (only match – amateur) 3 runs in only innings.

Played cricket for Sutton Coldfield and hockey for Sutton Coldfield and W.

SHAW, Dennis George – RHB LBG

b. Salford, Lancs., 16 February 1931. Educated at Queen Elizabeth's Grammar School, Walsall.

Debut 1949 v Services, Edgbaston (only match – professional). Highest score: W 17. Best bowling: W 2–60.

Played for Walsall (Birmingham League), Streetly. Later played for Vancouver CC (Canada).

SHILTON, John Edward – RHB SLA

b. Horbury Junction Railway Station, Yorks., 2 October 1861; d. Sedbergh, Yorks., 27 September 1899. Educated at Mirfield School.

Debut 1894 v Notts., Trent Bridge (played non-first-class from 1885; 143 consecutive W matches 1885–95). 19 matches for W 1894–95 (professional). Highest score: W 30 v Notts., Trent Bridge 1894. Best bowling: W 7–75 v Notts., Edgbaston 1894. Took 748 wickets (14.44) in all matches for W.

First-class debut North v South, Lord's 1884. Full first-class record 203 runs (9.23); 71 wickets (22.97). Played county cricket for Durham (1882), Northumberland

(1883), Yorks. (1883), Worcs. (1891). Played for Dudley, Salters' and West Bromwich Dartmouth in Birmingham League; numerous other professional engagements from 1881 (Mirfield) to Sedbergh CC and Sedbergh School in 1898.

Played for W under the identity of John Shilton, born Coventry 1857 (a first-cousin). In fact never resident in W long enough to have a proper qualification through 11-season service.

Autobiography *John Edward Shilton's Book* commenced 1879; unfinished. Completed, edited and published in third person, by Robert Brooke (1984).

SHORTLAND, Norman Arthur – RHB RM

b. Coventry, 6 July 1916; d. Finham, Coventry, 14 March 1973. Educated at Stoke School, Coventry.

Debut 1938 v Glam., Edgbaston. 23 matches for W 1938–50 (professional 1938–39, then amateur – cap 1946). Highest score: W 70 v Sussex, Edgbaston 1946.

Played for Coventry and North W.

Rugby Union for England schoolboys, Nuneaton, W. Uncle, Walter Duckham, played for Suffolk.

SHUCKBURGH, Sir Charles Gerald Stewkley (Baronet) – RHB

b. Shuckburgh, W, 28 February 1911; d. White Colne, nr Colchester, Essex 4 May 1988. Educated at Harrow and Trinity College, Oxford.

Debut 1930 v Notts., Edgbaston (only match – amateur) 0 in only innings.

Played variously for club sides – including I Zingari, Free Foresters, Leics. Gentlemen until 1950.

SIMMS, Harry Lester – RHB RFM

b. Adelaide, S. Australia, 31 January 1888; d. Weybridge, Surrey, 9 June 1942. Educated at Repton.

Debut 1921 v Northants, Edgbaston. 5 matches for W 1921–22 (amateur). Highest score: W 38, 2nd innings of debut. Best bowling: W 2–8 v Worcs., Edgbaston 1922.

79 matches for Sussex, 1905–13, also appeared first-class cricket in India 1909–10 to 1918–19. Highest first-class score 126 Sussex v Notts., Hove 1912. Best first-class bowling 7–84 Bombay Presidency v Parsis, Bombay, 1911–12. Performed the 'double' 1912; 1099 runs (20.73); 110 wickets (22.68). Full first-class record: 3154 runs (17.92); 220 wickets (19.31). Played for Aston Unity (Birmingham League).

SMALL, Gladstone Cleophas ('Gladys') – RHB RFM

b. St George, Barbados, 18 October 1961. Educated at Moseley Comprehensive School, Hall Green Technical College.

Debut 1980 v Hants, Southampton. 163 matches for W 1980–date (cap 1982). Highest score: W 70 v Lancs., Old Trafford 1988. Best bowling: W 7–15 v Notts., Edgbaston 1988.

5 Tests for England from 1986; 61 runs (15.25); 20 wickets (22.70). First-class debut for D.H. Robins' XI in New Zealand 1979–80; played for S. Australia 1985–86.

SMART, Cyril Cecil – RHB RM

b. Lacock, nr Chippenham, Wilts., 23 July 1898; d. Abertillery, S. Wales 21 May 1975.

Debut v Surrey, The Oval 1920. 45 matches for W 1920–22 (professional – cap

1922). Highest score: W 59 v Lancs., Edgbaston 1921. Best bowling: W 2–16 v Cambridge U, Edgbaston 1920.

Played for Glam. 1927–46; highest first-class score 151* Glam. v Sussex, Hastings 1936. Best first-class bowling 5–39 Glam. v Som., Weston-super-Mare 1939. Hit G. Hill (Hants) for 32 in one over (664664) Glam. v Hants., Cardiff 1935. Full first-class record; 8992 runs (26.68); 9 centuries; 180 wickets (41.69). Played for Griff & Coton CC.

Brother, Jack Smart, played for W; father, Tom Smart, played for Wilts.

SMART, John Abbott ('Jack') – RHB OB WK
b. Forest Hill, Marlborough, Wilts., 12 April 1891; d. Bedworth, 3 October 1979. Educated at Marlborough Church of England School.

Debut v Worcs., Edgbaston 1919. 238 matches for W 1919–36 (professional – cap

1922). Highest score: W 68* v Worcs., Stourbridge 1922. Best bowling: W 3–31 v Northants, Northampton 1922. 5 stumpings in match (W record) v Leics., Hinckley 1933. 79 dismissals in season (56 ct 23 st) 1932; W record until 1985.

First-class umpire 1937–48; stood in 4 Tests 1939–47. Professional and groundsman for Griff & Coton CC; scoreboard bears his name. Father, Tom Smart, played for Wilts and coach at Marlborough College; brother, Cyril Smart, played for W and Glam.

SMITH, Alan Christopher – RHB WK RMF
b. Hall Green, Birmingham, 25 October 1936. Educated at King Edward's School, Edgbaston, Brasenose College, Oxford.

Debut 1958 v Som., Taunton. 358 matches for W 1958–74 (amateur – cap 1961 – captain 1968–74). Highest score: W 94 v Middx., Coventry Courtaulds 1962. Best bowling: W 5–47 v Glam., Edgbaston 1972. Hat trick, W v Essex, Clacton 1965 (after starting match as wicketkeeper). W Secretary 1976–86.

6 matches for England 1962–63; scored 69* v New Zealand, Wellington 1962–63, adding 163 (unbroken) for 9th wicket with M.C. Cowdrey, English Test record for that wicket. 118 runs (29.50); 20 dismissals

(all caught) in Test cricket. Full first-class record: 11027 runs (20.92); 3 centuries; 131 wickets (23.46). Highest first-class score: 145 Oxford U v Hants, Bournemouth 1959 (scored 124 in 2nd innings). Best first-class bowling 5–32 (9–77) match) Oxford U v Free Foresters, Oxford 1960.

Secretary TCCB since 1986. Test selector 1969–73; 1982–86. Oxford Soccer Blue; some time director, Aston Villa AFC.

Derby., Edgbaston 1927. 800 dismissals (662 ct, 138 st) – W record. 7 dismissals (4 ct 3 st) v Derby., Edgbaston 1926; W record for innings. 1000 runs (6); 1461 (32.46) 1925 best. 121* at lunch, day 1, in innings of 134 v Hants, Coventry and North W 1912. 11 Tests for England 1911–12 to 1913–14; 20 dismissals (17 ct 3 st). Full first-class record: 16997 runs (22.39); 722 ct 156 st;

W Coaching Staff 1946 until death, part-time after 1963. First-class umpire 1931–39. Stood in 8 Tests 1933–39.

SMITH, David Martin – LHB SLA
b. Coventry, 21 January 1962. Educated at Caludon Castle, Coventry.

Debut 1981 v Hants, Edgbaston 1981. 4 matches for W 1981–83. Highest score: W 100* v Oxford U, Edgbaston 1983.

Played for Coventry and North W (Birmingham League), GEC (Coventry), Leamington.

SMITH, Ernest James ('Tiger') – RHB WK
b. Highgate, Birmingham, 6 February 1886; d. Northfield, Birmingham, 31 August 1979.

Debut 1904 v S. Africa, Edgbaston. 444 matches for W 1904–30 (professional – capped). Benefit (£700) 1922. Joint testimonial with George Austin (scorer) 1955; £898 each. Highest score: W 177 v

SMITH, Irving Wilmot – RHB RM/LB
b. Harborne, Birmingham, 5 February 1884; d. Sutton Coldfield, 21 October 1971. Educated at King Edward's School, Birmingham.

Debut 1905 v Yorks., Edgbaston (only match – amateur).

Highest score: W 1.

Played for Harborne CC.

SMITH, Kenneth David – RHB
b. Jesmond, Newcastle-upon-Tyne, 9 July 1956. Educated at Heaton Grammar School, Newcastle-upon-Tyne.

Debut 1973 v Cambridge U, Edgbaston. 196 matches for W 1973–85 (cap 1978). Highest score: W 140 v Worcs., Worcester 1980. 1000 runs (4); 1582 (36.79) 1980 best.

Played for Smethwick (Birmingham League).

Father, Kenneth D. Smith, played for Leics.; brother, Paul Smith, plays for W; father-in-law, Alan Oakman, played for Sussex and England, and W coach.

SMITH, Michael John Knight – RHB
b. Broughton Astley, Leics., 30 June 1933. Educated at Stamford, St Edmond Hall, Oxford.

Debut 1956 v Scotland, Edgbaston. 430 matches for W 1956–75 (amateur – cap 1957 – captain 1957–67). Highest score: W 200* v Worcs., Worcester 1959. Hit century against every other county. 1000 runs (16); 2417 (60.43) 1959 best (W record). 6 catches in innings, v Leics., Hinckley 1962 (county record); record 52 catches 1961; record 422 catches in career.

Played for Leics. 1951–55 (cap 1955). Played for Oxford U 1954–56 (Blue each season – captain 1956). 50 Tests for England 1958–72 (captain 25 times). 2278 runs in Tests (31.63); highest Test score 121 v S. Africa, Cape Town 1964–65. Best first-class score: 204, Cavaliers v Natal, Durban 1960–61. Full first-class record: 39832 runs (41.84); 69 centuries. 592 catches. Record aggregate for July – 1209 runs (93.00) in all first-class matches 1959.

Shares England Test record partnership for 7th wicket – 197 with J.M. Parks v W. Indies, Port-of-Spain 1959–60. Played for King's Heath.

W Committee since 1971. Awarded OBE for services to cricket. Rugby Union for Oxford (Blue), Leicester and England (1 cap). Son, N.M.K. Smith plays for W.

SMITH, Neil Michael Knight – RHB OB
b. Birmingham 27 July 1967. Educated at

M.J.K. Smith, captain (1957–67), hit a century against every other county

Warwick School.

Debut 1987 v Lancs., Southport. 3 matches for W 1987–date. Highest score: W 23 on debut. Best bowling: W 2–73 on debut.

Played for Leamington CC.

Father, M.J.K. Smith, played for W and England; great-grandfather, R.C. Leach, played for Lancs.

SMITH, Paul Andrew – RHB RFM
b. Jesmond, Newcastle-upon-Tyne, 15 April 1964. Educated at Heaton Grammar School, Newcastle-upon-Tyne.

Debut 1982 v Cambridge U, Cambridge. 128 matches for W 1982–date (cap 1986). Highest score: W 119 v Worcs., Edgbaston 1986. Best bowling: W 4–25 v Lancs., Edgbaston 1985. 1000 runs (2); 1431 (37.65) 1986 best. With Andy Moles shared in opening stands of 161 and 155 v Somerset, Weston-super-Mare 1986 – the only instance of two 1st wicket stands in excess of 150 for W. With Moles put on more than 50 for the first wicket in 8 consecutive innings during 1986.

Brother, K.D. Smith, played for W; father, Kenneth D. Smith, played for Leics.

SMITH, William John – RHB RFM
b. Freasley, near Wood End, North W, 13 May 1882; deceased. Nothing is known of this player after his only match for the county. He worked as a coal miner in the Polesworth area.

Debut 1906 v Hants, Edgbaston (only match – professional). Scored 0 in only innings. Best bowling: W 2–83.

Played for Polesworth and Freasley.

SNOW, John Augustine – RHB RF
b. Peopleton, Worcs., 13 October 1941.

Educated at Christ's Hospital, Horsham; Chichester High School and Culham Teacher Training College. Played 6 John Player Sunday League and 1 Gillette Cup Match W 1980.

267 matches for Sussex 1961–77 (cap 1964). Benefit (£18,000) 1974. 49 Tests for England 1965–76. 772 runs (13.54); 202 wickets (26.66). Highest Test and first-class score 73 v India, Lord's 1971; also scored 73* Sussex v Worcs., Worcester 1977. Best Test bowling: 7–40 v Australia, Sydney 1970–71. Best first-class bowling: 8–87 Sussex v Middx., Lord's 1975. Full first-class record: 4832 runs (14.17); 1174 wickets (22.72). Autobiography: *Cricket Rebel* (1976); two books of poetry – *Contrasts* (1971) and *Moments and Thoughts* (1973).

SPEED, Andrew Watson – RHB RFM
b. Glasgow, 19 January 1899.

Debut 1927 v Worcs., Worcester. 8 matches for W 1927–28 (amateur). Highest score: W 11* v Glam., Edgbaston 1928. Best bowling: W 6–81 v Glam., Cardiff 1928.

Played for Moseley (Birmingham League). At time of writing, the oldest known surviving W cricketer.

SPENCER, Harry Norman Ernest – RHB RM

b. Shipston-on-Stour, W, 1 October 1901; d. Hammersmith, London, 13 August 1954.

Debut 1930 v Worcs., Edgbaston. 3 matches for W 1930 (amateur). Highest score: W 3* on debut. Best bowling: W 1–44 on debut.

1 match for Worcs. 1927. Wicket with first ball for W. Played for Stratford-upon-Avon and Coventry and North W.

SPOONER, Richard Thompson ('Dick') – LHB WK

b. Stockton-on-Tees, Co. Durham 30 December 1919.

Debut 1948 v Notts., Trent Bridge. 312 matches for W 1948–59 (professional – cap 1948). Benefit (£3,784) 1957. Highest score: W 168 v Lancs., Old Trafford 1953. 1000 runs (6); 1767 (43.09) 1951 best. 682 dismissals for W – second to 'Tiger' Smith.

7 Tests for England 1951–52 to 1955; highest Test score 92 v India, Calcutta

1951–52. 354 Test runs (27.23); 10 ct 2 st. Full first-class career; 13851 runs (27.26) 12 centuries; 589 ct 178 st. Played for Durham Co. 1946–47; appeared for Norton-on-Tees, Knowle & Dorridge.

STEPHENS, Frank Garfield – RHB OB

b. Edgbaston, 26 April 1889; d. Moseley, Birmingham, 9 August 1970. Educated at Rossall.

Debut 1907 v Yorks., Sheffield. 32 matches for W 1907–12 (amateur). Highest score: W 144* v Lancs., Edgbaston 1912. Best bowling: W 2–24 v Yorks., Edgbaston 1907.

Played for Moseley in Birmingham League.

Twin brother, G.W. Stephens, also played for W and Moseley.

STEPHENS, George William – RHB LB

b. Edgbaston, 26 April 1889; d. Knowle, Solihull, 17 March 1950. Educated at Rossall.

Debut 1907 v Lancs., Old Trafford. 123 matches for W 1907–25 (amateur) – capped – county captain 1919). Highest score: W 143 v Glos., Edgbaston 1923. Best bowling: W 2–25 v Sussex, Hove 1913.

Played for Moseley in Birmingham League.

Twin brother, F.G. Stephens, played for W and Moseley.

STEVENSON, John Francis – RHB
b. Handsworth, Birmingham, 16 March 1888; d. Edgbaston, 5 December 1951. Educated at Benson Road School, Gib Heath, Birmingham.

Debut 1919 v Lancs., Old Trafford (only match – amateur). Highest score: W 18.

Played for Mitchells & Butlers (Birmingham League). Soccer: England schoolboys; on Birmingham books until 1912. Father, F.W. Stevenson, played for W pre-first-class.

STEWART, William James Perver – RHB
b. Llanelly, Carmarthenshire, S. Wales 31 August 1934.

Debut 1955 v Oxford U, Oxford 1955. 279 matches for W 1955–69 (professional – cap 1957). Benefit (£8,346) 1967. Highest score: W 182* v Leics., Hinckley 1962. Best bowling: W 2–4 v Sussex, Hove 1959. 1000 runs (6); 2318 (43.74) 1962 best. Hit 17 sixes in match (10 in first innings 155, 7 in second innings 125) v Lancs., Blackpool 1959. Also, 11 sixes in match (8 in first innings 104, 3 in second innings 55*) v Som., Street 1961. Century before lunch three times: 0–131* (eventual score 151), 1st morning, v Services, Portland Road 1959; 0–107* (eventual score 155) 2nd morning v Lancs., Blackpool 1959; 0–103* (eventual score 182*) 3rd morning v Leics., Hinckley 1962.

Played 1 match for Northants 1971. Toured New Zealand with MCC 1960–61. Suffered amputation of a big toe 1962–63. Rugby Union for Coventry and W; Welsh trialist.

STORIE, Alastair Caleb – RHB
b. Bishopbriggs, Glasgow, 25 July 1965. Educated at St Stithians College, Jo'burg.

Debut v Surrey, The Oval 1987. 25 matches for W 1987–88. Highest score: W 68 v Notts., Edgbaston 1968.

Played for Northants 1985–86; Orange Free State 1987–88. Highest first-class score 106 Northants v Hants, Northampton 1985 (first-class debut).

STREET, Lawrence Charles – RHB RFM
b. Erdington, Birmingham 4 February 1920. Educated at Moseley Grammar School.

Debut 1946 v Som., Edgbaston. 4 matches for W 1946 (professional). Highest score: W 8*, on debut. Best bowling: W 2–15 same match.
Played for Harborne Somerville, Harborne and Birmingham City Officials.

STREET, Norman Kingsley – RHB
b. Birmingham, 13 August 1881; d. in action, Suvla Bay, Gallipoli, 10 August 1915. Educated at Bromsgrove School.
Debut 1908 v Leics., Leicester. 5 matches for W 1908 (amateur). Highest score: W 14 v Surrey, Edgbaston 1908.
Regular Army officer (Worcs. Regiment); several years stationed in Malta limited cricket.

SUCKLING, Ernest – LHB SLA
b. Balsall Heath, Birmingham, 27 March 1890; d. Blackpool, 24 February 1962.
Debut 1919 v Yorks., Edgbaston. 2 matches for W 1919 (professional). Highest score: W 39 v Worcs., Edgbaston 1919.
3 matches for Worcs. 1923–24.
Club cricket for Sparkhill Belvedere, while living in Birmingham.

SUTCLIFFE, Simon Paul – RHB OB
b. Watford, Herts., 22 May 1960. Educated at Bedford Modern School, King George V Grammar School, Southport, Lincoln College Oxford and Loughborough College.
Debut 1981 v Som., Edgbaston. 20 matches for W 1981–83. Highest score: W

20 v Glos., Nuneaton Griff & Coton 1982.
Best bowling: W 5–151 v Essex, Colchester
1982.
  17 matches for Oxford U 1980–81 (Blue
both seasons). Best first-class bowling:
6–19 Oxford U v W, Oxford 1980. Played
for Mitchells & Butlers (Birmingham
League), Stratford-upon-Avon.
  Father, Peter Sutcliffe, former national
cricket coach.

SWARANJIT SINGH – LHB RM
b. Amritsar, N. Punjab, India, 18 July
1932. Educated at Khalsa College, Punjab
U, Christ's College, Cambridge.
  Debut 1956 v Scotland, Edgbaston.
Highest score: W 68* v Scotland,
Edgbaston 1957. Best bowling: W 5–132 v
Surrey, Edgbaston 1957.
  Played for Cambridge U 1954–56 (Blue
1955–56); East Punjab 1950–51 to 1958–59;
Bengal 1959–60 to 1961–62. Highest
first-class score: 145 E. Punjab v Delhi,
Delhi 1951–52; Best first-class bowling:
6–20 (10–63 match) Cambridge U v
Worcs., Worcester 1955. Played for
Moseley (Birmingham League). First-class
career record: 3684 runs (27.08); 183
wickets (29.65).

TATE, Cecil Frederick – RHB SLA
b. Gillingham, Kent, 1 May 1908. Educated at Tollington Park School, North London.

Debut 1931 v Yorks., Leeds. 7 matches for W 1931–33 (professional). Highest score: W 17 v Worcs., Dudley 1933. Best bowling: W 3–65 v Yorks., Edgbaston 1931.

4 matches for Derby. 1928. Played for West Bromwich Dartmouth (Birmingham League), Burton CC (1937–61).

Father, F.W. Tate, and brother, Maurice W. Tate, both played for England and Sussex.

TAYLER, Frederick Ernest – RHB
b. Aston Blank, nr Chedworth, Glos., 18 July 1889; d. Cold Aston, Glos., 30 April 1954. Educated at Wellingborough.

Debut 1910 v Leics., Coventry and North W. 4 matches for W 1910 (amateur). Highest score: W 44 on debut.

4 matches for Glos. 1911.

Brother, H.W. Tayler, played for Glos. and Glam.

TAYLOR, Albert Edward ('Tich') – RHB RM
b. Chilvers Coton, Nuneaton, 14 June 1894; d. Rotherham, Yorks., 19 August 1960. Educated at Chilvers Coton School.

Debut 1927 v Som., Taunton (only match – professional). Dismissed for 0, only innings.

Played for Chilvers Coton and Courtaulds (Coventry).

TAYLOR, Arthur – RHB RMF
b. Maltby, Yorks. 1880; d. Winson Green, Birmingham, 13 November 1956.

Debut 1913 v Sussex, Coventry and North W 1913. 6 matches for W 1913 (professional). Highest score: W 17 v Yorks., Sheffield 1913. Best bowling: W 2–10 on debut. Played for Leamington CC.

Groundsman at Edgbaston several years either side of WWI.

TAYLOR, Charles James – RHB RFM
b. Bristol, 8 June 1881; d. Leek, Staffs., August 1960.

Debut 1908 v Hants, Portsmouth. 3 matches for W 1908–09 (professional).

b. Birkenhead, Cheshire, 3 October 1951.
Educated at Birkenhead School and
Trinity College, Cambridge.

Debut 1970 v Cambridge U, Edgbaston
(only match); did not bat.

Played for Cambridge U 1971–73, Blue
each season. 2 matches for Middx. 1981;
first match v Essex was not registered, and
Middx. were penalised 7 points. Played for
Cheshire 1969–70; club: Oxton.

Highest score: W 5 v Yorks., Edgbaston
1909. Best bowling: W 4–99 same match.

Also played for Staffs., and various N.
Staffs. clubs.

Son, Fred Taylor, played for W and
Staffs.

TAYLOR, Chilton Richard Vernon – RHB
WK

TAYLOR, Derief David Samuel – LHB
SLA
b. Kingston, Jamaica, 17 September, c
1908; d. Kingston, Jamaica, 15 March
1987.

Debut 1948 v Oxford U, Oxford 1948. 16
matches for W 1948–50 (professional).
Highest-score: W 121 v Leics., Edgbaston
1949. Best bowling: W 3–41 v Hants,
Edgbaston 1948. W Juniors' coach
1951–81.

Played for West Bromwich Dartmouth
(Birmingham League).

Junior Soccer referee in Birmingham
area.

TAYLOR, Donald Dougal – RHB OB
b. Auckland, New Zealand, 2 March 1923;
d. Auckland, New Zealand, 5 April 1980.
Educated at Mount Albert Grammar
School, Auckland.

Debut 1949 v Oxford U, Edgbaston. 45 matches for W 1949–53 (professional). Highest score: W 90* v Notts., Trent Bridge 1951. Best bowling: W 4–24 v Services, Edgbaston 1949.

Played for Auckland 41 times between 1946–47 and 1960–61. 3 Tests for New Zealand 1946–47 to 1955–56. Highest Test score 77 v W. Indies, Wellington 1955–56. Test record: 159 runs (31.80). Full first-class record: 3734 runs (23.63); 30 wickets (33.96). Played in Birmingham League Old Hill and West Bromwich Dartmouth. Added 220 and 286 for 1st wicket with B. Sutcliffe, Auckland v Canterbury, Auckland, 1948–49; the only instance of two double-century 1st wicket stands in a first-class match by one team.

Edgbaston 1947. 1259 runs (26.22) in 1947. Clubs: N. Middx., Notts Forest. Notts. cricket manager from 1979.

TAYLOR, Frederick – RHB RFM
b. Leek, Staffs., 29 April 1916. Educated at Leek Council School.

Debut 1939 v Cambridge U, Portland Road (only match – professional). Scored 0 in only innings. Best bowling: W 2–56.

Played for Staffs. 1937–38; 1946–51. First-class match for Minor Counties v Australia, Stoke 1953. Appeared for N. Staffs. clubs Burslem, Knypersley, Porthill Park, Leek, Stone.

Father, C.J. Taylor, played for W and Staffs.

TAYLOR, Kenneth Alexander – RHB RM
b. Muswell Hill, London, 29 September 1916. Educated at Tollington Park School, N. London.

Debut 1946 v Sussex, Edgbaston. 87 matches for W 1946–49 (professional – cap 1946). Highest score: W 102 v Glos.,

TEDSTONE, Geoffrey Alan – RHB WK
b. Southport, Lancs., 19 January 1961. Educated at Warwick School and St Paul's College, Cheltenham.

Debut 1982 v Oxford U, Oxford. 32 matches for W 1982–88. Highest score: W 67* v Cambridge U, Cambridge 1983.

Not re-engaged after 1988 but taken on part-time coaching staff. Sister, Janet Tedstone, played for England Women.

School, Birmingham.

Debut 1978 v Lancs., Old Trafford. 8 matches for W 1978–81. Highest score: W 52 v Yorks., Scarborough 1981.

Played for Boland (S. Africa) 1987–88. Full first-class record 377 runs (19.84). Played for Mitchells & Butlers (Birmingham League).

TENNANT, Peter Norie – RHB WK
b. Sutton Coldfield, 17 April 1942. Educated at Solihull School.

Debut 1964 v Scotland, Edgbaston (only match) did not bat.

Played for Aston Unity and Moseley in Birmingham League.

THOMPSON, John Ross – RHB RM
b. Berkhamstead, Herts., 10 May 1918. Educated at Tonbridge and St John's College, Cambridge.

Debut 1938 v Sussex, Portland Road. 44 matches for W 1938–54 (amateur – cap 1947). Highest score: W 103 v Som., Taunton 1949.

Played for Cambridge U 1938–39, Blue each season. Highest first-class score: 191 v Free Foresters, Cambridge 1938. Full first-class record: 3455 runs (31.12). Played for Wilts. 1955–63. Club cricket for Solihull.

British Amateur Squash Champion 1954–59; British Open Champion 1959.

THOMPSON, Roland George ('Roly') – RHB RFM
b. Binley Village, Coventry, 26 September 1932. Educated at Binley School, Coventry.

Debut 1949 v Worcs., Edgbaston. 158 matches for W 1949–62 (professional – cap 1955). Highest score: W 25*, v Notts., Trent Bridge 1956, and v Glos., Coventry

THOMAS, Gary Philip – RHB
b. Birmingham, 8 November 1958. Educated at George Dixon Grammar

Courtaulds 1961. Best bowling: W 9–65 v Notts., Edgbaston 1952. Hat trick v Sussex, Horsham 1956.

Played for Moseley (Birmingham League), Coventry and North W, Lockheed (Leamington).

Career curtailed by injury.

THORNE, David Anthony – RHB LM
b. Coventry, 12 December 1964. Educated at Bablake School, Coventry and Keble College, Oxford.

Debut 1983 v Oxford U, Edgbaston. 38 matches for W 1983–88. Highest score: W 76 v Worcs., Worcester 1988.

Played for Oxford U 1984–86 (Blue each season – captain 1986). Highest first-class score: 124 Oxford U v Zimbabwe, Oxford 1985. Best first-class bowling: 5–39 Oxford U v Cambridge U, Lord's 1984.

TIDY, Warwick Nigel – RHB LBG
b. Birmingham, 10 February 1953. Educated at John Wilmott Grammar School, Sutton Coldfield.

Debut 1970 v Oxford U, Oxford. 36 matches for W 1970–74. Highest score: 12* v Cambridge U, Cambridge 1972. Best bowling: W 5–24 v Leics., Nuneaton Griff & Coton 1970.

Played for Old Hill (Birmingham League), Walmley, Stratford-upon-Avon.

TIMMS, Bryan Stanley Valentine – RHB WK
b. Ropley, Hants, 17 December 1940.

Debut 1969 v Northants, Edgbaston 1969. 24 matches for W 1969–71 (cap 1971). Highest score: W 61 v Essex, Leyton 1969.

Played for Hants 1959–68 (cap 1963). Highest first-class score: 120 Hants v

Oxford U, Oxford 1966. Full first-class record: 3657 runs (15.76); 456 ct 70 st.

TOWNSEND, Alan – RHB RM
b. Stockton-on-Tees, Co. Durham, 26 August 1921.

Debut v Notts., Trent Bridge 1948. 340 matches for W 1948–60 (professional – cap 1948). Benefit (£4,143) 1960. Highest score: W 154 v Worcs., Dudley 1957. Best bowling: W 7–84 v Essex, Brentwood 1949. 1000 runs (5); 1201 (27.29) in 1957 best. 42 catches 1953, 41 catches 1951; both W records at the time. 409 catches for W – County record until beaten by M.J.K. Smith. Played for Durham County 1947, Mitchells & Butlers (Birmingham League), Thornaby, Eppleton.

Assistant coach, Edgbaston since 1982.

TUDOR, Richard Thornhill – RHB RM
b. Shrewsbury, Salop, 27 September 1948. Educated at Shrewsbury.

Debut 1976 v Cambridge U, Cambridge (only match). Highest score: W 6.

Played for Salop, 1975–77.

Club: Shrewsbury.

Warwickshire's top batsmen of 1959. Left to right: B. Ibadulla, A. Townsend, A.V.G. Wolton, M.J.K. Smith, T.W. Cartwright, W.J.P. Stewart and N.F. Horner

VENN, Horace – RHB
b. Coventry, 4 July 1892; d. Keresley, Coventry, 23 November 1953.

Debut 1919 v Worcs., Edgbaston. 34 matches for W 1919–25 (amateur). Highest score: W 151 on debut (highest score on first-class debut by a W player).

Played for various Coventry clubs, including Coventry and North W., Foleshill, Humber.

W

WALKER, Gilbert – RHB
b. Olton, Solihull, 15 February 1888; d. Mayborough, Victoria, Australia, c 1938.

Debut 1912 v Sussex, Edgbaston (only match – amateur). Highest score: 13.

Played for Olton CC, Mayborough CC.

Last heard of in Melbourne, Australia c 1924.

WADDY, Ernest Frederick – RHB RM
b. Morpeth, New South Wales, 5 October 1880; d. Evesham, Worcs. 23 September 1958. Educated at Sydney U.

Debut 1919 v Derby., Edgbaston. 26 matches for W 1919–22 (amateur – capped). Highest score: 109* v Middx., Lord's 1921.

Played for New South Wales 1902–03 to 1910–11. Toured Ceylon with his own XI 1913–14 (probably not first-class). Probable first-class record: 2326 runs (28.36). Highest first-class score: 129* New South Wales v S. Australia, Adelaide 1904–05.

A Church of England priest, came to England to be vicar of High Littleton, near Evesham, W. Played for Rugby CC. Brothers: E.L. Waddy (New South Wales) and P.S. Waddy (Oxford U). Nephew: B.B. Waddy (Oxford U).

WALL, Stephen – RHB RMF
b. Ulverston, Lancs., 10 December 1959.

Educated at Dondales School.

Debut 1984 v Leics., Leicester. 19 matches for W 1984–85. Highest score: W 28 v Lancs., Old Trafford 1985, and v Northants, Edgbaston 1985. Best bowling: W 4–48 v Derby., Chesterfield 1985.

Played for Cumberland since 1983.

WARD, Leslie Maynard – RHB RM OB

b. Coventry, 2 May 1908; d. Bideford, Devon, 13 January 1981. Educated at Bablake School, Coventry.

Debut 1930 v Leics., Hinckley (amateur – only match). Highest score: 5 (only innings).

Played for Coventry and North W.

Rugby Union for Coventry.

WARD, William – LHB SLA

b. Smethwick, Staffs., 24 May 1874; d. Birmingham, 28 December 1961.

Debut 1895 v Hants, Edgbaston. 11 matches for W 1895–1904 (professional). Highest score: W 26 v Cambridge U, Edgbaston 1904. Best bowling: W 5–76 v Surrey, The Oval 1896.

Played for King's Heath CC; subsequently a professional in the north of England.

WARING, John Shaw – RHB RFM

b. Ripon, Yorks., 1 October 1942.

Debut 1967 v Scotland, Edgbaston (only match – professional). Highest score: 15. Best bowling: 1–30.

Played for Yorks. 1963–66. Highest first-class score: 26 Yorks v Middx., Lord's 1966. Best first-class bowling: 7–40 Yorks. v Lancs., Leeds 1966. Full first-class record: 55 wickets (22.74). Played for Cumberland 1970–73; clubs included Leeds, Bingley, Kendal.

WARNER, Graham Sydney – RHB OB

b. Darlaston, Staffs., 27 November 1945. Educated at Darlaston Grammar School.

Debut 1966 v Oxford U, Edgbaston. 30 matches for W 1966–71. Highest score: W 118* v Scotland, Edgbaston 1968.

Played for Staffs. since 1976 to date. Appeared in Birmingham League for Smethwick and Mitchells & Butlers.

WASSALL, Albert – LHB SLA

b. Aston, Birmingham, 14 June 1892; d. Erdington, Birmingham, September 1975.

Debut 1923 v Hants, Portsmouth. 7 matches for W 1923 (professional). Highest score: W 10 on debut. Best bowling: W 3–67 v Glos., Bristol 1923.

Played for Aston Orient CC and HP Sauce CC.

WATSON, Thomas Herman – RHB RFM
b. Water Orton, 14 November 1880; d. Singleton, Blackpool, Lancs., 15 February 1944. Educated at St Bees and Pembroke College, Cambridge.

Debut 1904 v Yorks., Edgbaston. 2 matches for W 1904 (amateur). Highest score: W 12 v Cambridge U, Edgbaston 1904.

1 match for Cambridge U 1903. Played for Coleshill CC.

Father was vicar of Water Orton.

WATSON SMITH, Harry – RHB WK
b. Chesterfield, Derby., 30 September 1886; d. Ruthin, Denbighs., 24 June 1955.

Debut 1912 v Derby., Derby (only match – amateur). Scored 15 in only innings.

One match for Derby. 1920.

Played for Nuneaton CC while a mining engineer in North W. Coalfield.

WEBSTER, Rudi Valentine – RHB RFM
b. St Philip, Barbados, 10 June 1939. Educated at Edinburgh U.

Debut 1962 v Cambridge U, Cambridge. 60 matches for W 1962–66 (amateur – cap 1963). Highest score: W 47 v Glam., Edgbaston 1966. Best bowling: W 8–19 v Cambridge U, Cambridge 1966. Innings analysis: 7–6, match figures 12–58, W v Yorks., Edgbaston 1964.

Played for Scotland 1961–64; Otago 1966–67 and 1967–68. Took wicket with first ball in first-class cricket, and with first ball of 2nd innings of debut match, Scotland v MCC, Greenock 1961.

A medical practitioner specialising in children's diseases.

WEEKS, Raymond Thomas – LHB SLA
b. Camborne, Cornwall, 30 April 1930.

Debut 1950 v Cambridge U, Edgbaston. 105 matches for W 1950–57 (professional – cap 1951). Highest score: W 51 v Services, Edgbaston 1951. Best bowling: W 7–70 v Notts., Trent Bridge 1951. 94 wickets (21.75) in 1951.

Appeared for Corn. 1947–49; 1960–65. Played for West Bromwich Dartmouth in Birmingham League and Camborne.

WELDRICK, George – RHB
b. Brighouse, Yorks., 11 January 1882; d. Brighouse, 14 April 1953.

Debut 1906 v Yorks., Edgbaston. 8 matches for W 1906–07 (professional).

Highest score: W 12 v S. Africa, 1907.
Played for various Yorks. clubs, including Brighouse.

WELFORD, James William – RHB
b. Barnard Castle, Co. Durham, 27 March 1869; d. Glasgow, Scotland, 17 January 1945.

Debut 1896 v Surrey, The Oval. 13 matches for W 1896 (professional). Highest score: W 118 v Leics., Leicester 1896.

Played for Durham 1891–95; League cricket for Stockton, Barnard Castle and Bishop Auckland.

Soccer for Aston Villa and Glasgow Celtic.

WHEATLEY, Oswald Stephen ('Ossie') – RHB RMF
b. Low Fell, Gateshead, Co. Durham, 28 May 1935. Educated at King Edward's School, Edgbaston, Birmingham and Gonville & Caius College, Cambridge.

Debut 1957 v Services, Portland Road. 63 matches for W 1957–60 (amateur – cap 1959). Highest score: W 17 v Sussex, Edgbaston 1959. Best bowling: W 7–45 v Lancs., Old Trafford 1960 (match figures 10–107). 110 wickets (24.84) 1960.

First-class debut for Free Foresters 1956; Cambridge U 1957–58 (Blue both seasons) 80 wickets (17.63) in 1958, a record for either U. Played for Glam. 1961–70 (cap 1961; captain 1961–66). Highest first-class score: 34* Gents v Players, Scarborough 1961. Best first-class bowling: 9–60 Glam. v Sussex, Ebbw Vale 1968. First-class career record: 1099 wickets (20.84). Played for Harborne CC.

Test selector 1973–74. Glam. Chairman from 1977.

WHITE, Allan Frederick Tinsdale – RHB
b. Coventry, 5 September 1915. Educated at Uppingham and Pembroke College,

Cambridge.
Debut 1936 v Surrey, Edgbaston. 9 matches for W 1936–37 (amateur). Highest score: W 55* on debut.

Played for Cambridge U 1936–37 (Blue 1936); 110 matches for Worcs. 1939–49 (cap 1946 – captain 1947–48 – joint-captain 1949 with R.E.S. Wyatt). Highest first-class score: 95 Worcs. v Services, Worcester 1946. Played for Moseley (Birmingham League).

WHITE, Henry Albert – RHB OB RM
b. Watford, Herts., 8 August 1895; d. Barrow Gurney, Som. 27 November 1972.
Debut 1923 v Northants, Northampton. 8 matches for W 1923 (professional).

Highest score: W 32 on debut.
Played for Aston Unity (Birmingham League).

Soccer for Arsenal, Blackpool and Walsall. Father, Harry E. White, played for Herts., and later became head groundsman at Lord's 1910–36.

WHITE, Malcolm Frank – RHB WK
b. Walsall, Staffs., 15 May 1924. Educated at Queen Mary's Grammar School, Walsall and Magdalene College, Cambridge.
Debut 1946 v Derby., Edgbaston (only match – amateur). 0 runs, either innings.
Played for Staffs. 1954. Birmingham League for Walsall. Wartime Cambridge Blue (1944).

WHITEHEAD, James George – LHB LMF
b. Cape Town, S. Africa 1877; d. Mowbray, Cape Town, 23 January 1940.
Debut 1902 v London County, Crystal Palace (only match – professional). 1 run in only innings.
Played for Western Province and Griqualand West from 1904–05 to 1920–21. Best bowling in first-class cricket 7–58 W. Province v Natal, Cape Town 1907–08. Was professional/coach Cape Town CC. Played for Aston Unity in Birmingham League.

WHITEHEAD, Stephen James ('Jim') –
RHB RM OB
b. Enfield Highway, Enfield, Middx., 2
September 1860; d. Small Heath,
Birmingham 9 June 1904 (of English
cholera the day after attending benefit
match, v Essex).

Debut 1894 v Notts., Trent Bridge
(non-first-class since 1889). 55 matches for
W 1894–1900 (professional – capped).
Joint-benefit (£200 each) with Walter
Richards 1904. Highest score: W 46* v
Leics., Leicester 1894. Best bowling: W
8–47 on County first-class debut.

First-class cricket for Liverpool and
District 1891–92. Played for West
Bromwich Dartmouth (Birmingham
League) and Small Heath.

WHITEHOUSE, John – RHB Slow bowler
– right arm or left arm.
b. Nuneaton, 8 April 1949. Educated at
King Edward VI School, Nuneaton and
Bristol U.

Debut 1971 v Oxford U, Oxford. 179
matches for W 1971–80 (cap 1973 – captain
1978–79). Highest score: W 197 v Glam.
Edgbaston 1980. Best bowling: W 2–55 v
Yorks., Edgbaston 1977. 1000 runs (3);
1543 (42.86) 1977 best. Scored 173 on
first-class debut, going from 20* to 150* on
2nd morning. On W Committee since
1984.

Plays for Nuneaton.

WHITEHOUSE, Percy Gilbert – RHB RM
OB
b. Edgbaston, 1 August 1893; d. Copt

Heath, Solihull, 24 September 1959.

Debut 1926 v Kent, Tunbridge Wells. 3 matches for W 1926 (amateur). Highest score: W 13 v Hants, Portsmouth. Best bowling: W 4–23 v Glam., Swansea 1926. W Committee 1942–59.

Played for Harborne CC.

WHITTLE, Albert Edward Mark ('Bert') – RHB RM
b. Bristol, 16 September 1877; d. Charminster, Dorset, 18 March 1917.

Debut 1900 v London County, Crystal Palace. 60 matches for W 1900–06 (professional). Highest score: W 104 v Essex, Edgbaston 1904. Best bowling: W 5–28 v Leics., Leicester 1904. When obtaining best score above, added 181 with Billy Quaife, County 8th wicket record until 1925.

Played for Som. 1907–11. Full first-class record: 2552 runs (22.00); 64 wickets (37.82). Professional with Olton CC; scored 100* and took all 10 wickets in innings for 51 Olton v Yardley, Olton 1901 (his benefit match).

Originally came to W for trial with Aston Villa FC.

WILLIAMS, Owen Leslie – RHB SLA
b. Cape Town, S. Africa, 8 April 1948.

Debut 1967 v Scotland, Edgbaston (only match). Highest score: W 6.* Best

bowling: W 1–32.

Played for Aston Unity (Birmingham League).

Coach at Edgbaston Indoor Cricket School.

WILLIAMS, Rowland Powell – RHB
b. Stratford-upon-Avon, 8 January 1872; d. Yelverton, Buckland Monachorum, Devon, 16 December 1951. Educated at King Edward's School, Camp Hill, Birmingham.

Debut 1897 v Philadelphians, Edgbaston 1897. 5 matches for W 1897–98 (amateur). Highest score: W 38 v Glos., Gloucester 1897.

Other first-class matches for London County (1902) and Gentlemen (1905).

WILLIS, Robert George Dylan – RHB RF
b. Sunderland, Co. Durham, 30 May 1949. Educated at Guildford Royal Grammar School.

Debut 1972 v Australia, Edgbaston. 136 matches for W 1972–84 (cap 1972 – captain 1980–84). Benefit (£44,951) 1981. Highest score: W 72 v India, Edgbaston 1982. Best bowling: W 8–32 v Glos., Bristol 1977. Achieved two hat tricks – v Derby., Edgbaston 1972 and v W. Indies, Edgbaston 1976. Member of W Committee 1981–87.

34 matches for Surrey 1969–71; played for N. Transvaal 1972–73. 90 Tests for

England 1970–71 to 1984; captain 18 times. Highest Test score: 28* v Pakistan, Edgbaston 1982 and 28 v India, Lord's 1982. Best Test bowling: 8–43 v Australia, Leeds 1981. Test record: 840 runs (11.50); 325 wickets (25.20). Full first-class record: 2690 runs (14.30); 899 wickets (24.99).

Awarded MBE for services to cricket.

WILMOT, Kilburn ('Kil') – RHB RFM
b. Chilvers Coton, Nuneaton, 3 April 1911. Educated at Coton C of E School, Nuneaton.

Debut 1931 v Derby, Edgbaston. 75 matches for W 1931–39 (professional – capped). Highest score: W 54 v Derbys., Edgbaston 1939. Best bowling: W 7–34 v Surrey, The Oval 1936.

Played for Griff & Coton and Chilvers Coton Clubs. Soccer for Coventry City and Walsall.

WILSON, Ben Ambler – LHB SLA
b. Harrogate, Yorks. 22 September 1921; Educated at Harrogate Grammar School.

Debut 1951 v Scotland, Edgbaston (only match – professional). No runs. Best bowling: W 1–75.

Played for Suffolk 1955–59.

Clubs include Spen Victoria and Cupar (Scotland). Appointed professional/coach Blundell's School 1963. Father, Benjamin B. Wilson, played for Yorks.

WINDRIDGE, James Edwin – RHB RM
b. Sparkbrook, Birmingham, 21 October 1882; d. Small Heath, Birmingham, 23 September 1939.

Debut 1909 v Sussex, Edgbaston. 7 matches for W 1909–13 (professional). Highest score: W 34* v Yorks., Edgbaston 1912. Best bowling: W 1–13 v Leics., Edgbaston 1909.

Birmingham Parks cricket for Small Heath and Star of Hope.

Soccer for Chelsea, Middlesbrough and Birmingham. Cousin to Albert Bird (Worcs.), 'Professor' Billy Bird (W pre-first-class), Jack Leake (W pre-first-class), Albert Leake (Aston Villa and England soccer player).

WOLTON, Albert Victor George – RHB OB
b. Maidenhead, Berks., 12 June 1919. Educated at Holyport School.

Debut 1947 v Scotland, Edgbaston. 296

matches for W 1947–60 (professional) – cap 1949). Benefit (£3,543) 1959. 1000 runs (7); 1809 runs (34.13) 1955 best. Highest score: W 165 v Worcs., Dudley 1954. Best bowling: W 4–15 v Middx., Edgbaston 1953.

Played for Aston Unity, Mitchells & Butlers and West Bromwich Dartmouth in Birmingham; also Bray (Berkshire), King's Heath, Berks Gents.

WOODROFFE, Alfred – LHB
b. Birmingham, 1 September 1918; d.

Sutton Coldfield, 23 July 1964.

Debut 1947 v Worcs., Dudley. 4 matches for W 1947–48 (professional). Highest score: W 41 v Glos., Edgbaston 1947.

Played for Aston Unity (Birmingham League).

WOOTTON, Simon Howard – LHB LM
b. Perivale, Middx., 24 February 1959. Educated at Arthur Terry School, Sutton Coldfield.

Debut 1981 v Sri Lanka, Edgbaston. 11 matches for W 1981–83. Highest score: W 104 v Cambridge U, Cambridge 1983.

4 matches for Glos. 1984. Full first-class record: 558 runs (26.57). Played for Lichfield, Stratford-upon-Avon, Stourbridge, Moseley (Birmingham League).

Father, B.A. Wootton, celebrated wicketkeeper in London Club Cricket (Headstone CC); brother-in-law, Alan Lee (cricket correspondent, *The Times*).

WRIGHT, Albert – RHB RM
b. Arley, nr Nuneaton, 25 August 1941.

Debut 1960 v Oxford U, Portland Road. 76 matches for W 1960–64 (professional –

cap 1962). Highest score: W 27 v Glam.,
Edgbaston 1961. Best bowling: W 6–58 v
Surrey, Edgbaston 1962. 116 wickets
(21.31) 1962.

Played for Mitchells & Butlers
(Birmingham League); later professional
in South Wales.

WYATT, Robert Elliott Storey – RHB
RMF
b. Milford, Surrey, 2 May 1901. Educated
at King Henry VIII School, Coventry.

Debut 1923 v Worcs., Edgbaston. 404
matches for W 1923–39 (amateur cap 1923
– captain 1930–37). Highest score: W 232 v
Derby., Edgbaston 1937. Best bowling: W
7–43 v Middx., Lord's 1926. 1000 runs
(12); 2075 (61.03) 1928 best. Added 228
with A.J.W. Croom v Worcs., Dudley

1925; county record for 8th wicket.

Played for Worcs 1946–51 (cap 1946;
joint-captain with A.F.T. White 1949,
captain 1950–51). 40 Tests for England
1927–28 to 1936–37 (captain on 16
occasions). Test record 1839 runs (31.70);
18 wickets (35.68). Full first-class record;
39405 runs (40.04); 901 wickets (32.84).
Final first-class match for Free Foresters in
1957 aged 56. Played for Moseley
(Birmingham League), Meriden.

Test selector: 1949–53 (Chairman 1950).
Autobiography, *Three Straight Sticks*
(1961).

R.E.S. Wyatt, captain (1930–37)

YOULL, Michael – LHB SLA
b. Newcastle-upon-Tyne, Northumberland, 26 April 1939. Educated at Heanor Grammar School.

Debut 1956 v Scotland, Edgbaston. 4 matches for W 1956–57 (professional). Highest score: W 9 v Services, Portland Road 1957. Best bowling: W 5–99 on debut.

Played for Northumberland 1962–81.

A cartoonist's depiction of J.H.G. Devey

First-Class Career Records

Name	Seasons	Match	Inns	N.O.	Runs	H.S.	100	Av'ge	Runs	Wts	Av'ge	Ct/st
Abberley, R.N.	1964–79	258	433	27	9825	117*	3	24.19	294	5	58.80	170
Abell, R.B.	1967	1	—	—	—	—	—	—	112	4	28.00	1
Adderley, C.H.	1946	5	8	2	27	12	—	4.50	255	4	63.75	1
Allan, J.M.	1966–68	48	58	17	744	76*	—	18.14	2274	58	39.20	19
Amiss, D.L.	1960–87	547	946	102	35146	232*	78	41.64	560	15	37.33	352
Asif Din, M.	1981–	141	227	35	5837	158*	5	30.40	2899	50	57.98	80
Austin, H.	1919	4	6	2	45	13	—	11.25	234	2	117.00	2
Bainbridge, H.W.	1894–1902	118	186	16	4973	162	6	29.25	36	1	—	73
Baker, C.S.	1905–20	214	355	42	9244	155*	10	29.53	1017	22	46.22	98
Banks, D.A.	1988–	7	9	1	195	61	—	24.37	—	—	—	—
Bannister, J.D.	1950–68	368	448	120	3080	71	—	9.39	25918	1181	21.94	167
Barber, E.G.	1936	2	3	0	31	13	—	10.33	—	—	—	2
Barber, R.W.	1963–69	124	214	11	5978	138	5	29.44	4854	197	24.63	80
Barber, W.H.	1927–33	5	6	1	71	23	—	14.20	253	7	36.14	1
Barbery, A.E.	1906–07	2	3	0	13	6	—	4.33	245	3	81.66	—
Barker, M.P.	1946	5	9	2	55	17	—	7.85	378	16	23.62	1
Barnes, S.F.	1894–96	4	6	2	38	18	—	9.50	199	3	66.33	3
Barnes, T.P.	1956	1	1	0	7	7	—	—	—	—	—	1
Barton, J.	1895–96	3	4	0	38	16	—	9.50	165	7	23.57	—
Bates, L.T.A.	1913–35	440	745	53	19326	211	21	27.92	471	9	52.33	154
Bates, S.H.	1910–12	5	9	1	24	13	—	3.00	182	6	30.33	—
Bayley, M.G.	1969	2	2	1	2	1*	—	—	125	3	41.66	2
Baynton, R.G.	1921–23	13	19	1	212	36	—	11.77	479	14	34.21	3
Benjamin, H.L.	1919	2	3	0	35	23	—	11.66	130	2	65.00	—
Benjamin, J.E.	1988	1	—	—	—	—	—	—	53	0	—	—
Benson, G.L.	1959–61	3	5	2	102	46	—	34.00	32	2	16.00	1
Blenkiron, W.	1964–74	117	137	30	1455	62	—	13.59	8094	287	28.20	55
Bourne, W.A.	1973–77	59	76	13	1300	107	1	20.63	4074	126	32.33	38
Breeden, C.L.	1910	5	8	1	80	27	—	11.42	29	0	—	4
Brewster, V.C.	1965	2	4	1	58	35*	—	19.33	175	10	17.50	1
Bridge, W.B.	1955–68	98	131	33	1057	56*	—	10.78	7363	281	26.20	59
Brindle, R.G.	1949	1	2	0	74	42	—	37.00	—	—	—	—
Broberg, R.F.	1920	1	1	0	4	4	—	—	16	0	—	—
Bromley, P.H.	1947–56	49	66	11	1183	121*	1	21.50	1264	35	36.11	37
Brown, A.	1932	1	1	1	1	1*	—	—	96	2	48.00	1
Brown, D.J.	1961–82	325	370	99	3240	79	—	11.95	24078	1005	23.95	139
Brown, E.	1932–34	28	29	9	134	19*	—	6.70	1877	56	33.51	10
Brown, J.D.	1913-14	9	12	5	12	7	—	1.71	264	9	29.33	4
Buckingham, J	1933–39	93	142	23	2840	137*	3	23.86	—	—	—	133/91
Burton, R.H.M.	1919	1	1	0	47	47	—	—	—	—	—	—
Busher, H.A.	1908	1	2	1	15	15	—	—	—	—	—	—
Byrne, G.R.	1912	8	12	0	36	11	—	3.00	84	6	14.00	1
Byrne, J.F.	1897–1912	138	215	10	4730	222	4	23.07	2123	71	29.90	80
Cannings, V.H.D.	1947–49	53	77	25	745	61	—	14.32	2914	88	33.11	12
Carter. R.G.	1951–61	88	109	20	635	37	—	7.13	6699	241	27.79	42
Cartwright, T.W.	1952–69	353	558	70	10781	210	5	22.09	19838	1058	18.75	262
Charlesworth, C.	1898–1921	372	632	27	14289	216	15	23.61	8878	294	30.19	194
Clarkson, W.	1922–23	2	4	0	59	41	—	14.75	52	2	26.00	—
Claughton, J.A.	1979–80	18	30	5	545	108*	2	21.80	—	—	—	6
Clifford, C.C.	1978–80	36	33	12	171	26	—	8.14	4074	100	40.74	11

207

Name	Seasons	Match	Inns	N.O.	Runs	H.S.	100	Av'ge	Runs	Wts	Av'ge	Ct/st
Clugston, D.L.	1928–46	6	9	0	64	17	—	7.11	475	4	118.75	3
Collin, T.	1933–36	52	75	7	1399	105*	1	20.57	1302	26	50.07	35
Cook, D.R.	1962–68	9	13	5	108	28*	—	13.50	534	23	23.21	7
Cook, M.S.	1961–62	2	4	0	110	52	—	27.50	—	—	—	—
Cooke, R.	1925–26	15	21	4	66	14	—	3.88	507	16	31.68	6
Cordner, J.P.	1952	1	—	—	—	—	—	—	36	0	—	—
Cotton, R.H.	1947	2	3	1	0	0*	—	0.00	128	2	64.00	—
Cowan, C.F.R.	1909–21	27	49	2	735	78	—	15.63	9	0	—	9
Cranmer, P.	1934–54	166	268	13	5595	113	4	21.94	1098	22	49.90	122
Crawford, A.B.	1911	7	10	3	140	40	—	20.00	310	13	23.84	2
Cresswell, J.	1895–99	15	22	9	137	16	—	10.54	1144	42	27.23	12
Crichton, H.T.	1908	2	3	0	26	26	—	8.66	30	2	15.00	—
Crockford, E.B.	1911–22	21	35	0	394	55	—	11.26	199	2	99.50	6
Croom, A.J.W.	1922–39	394	622	65	17662	211	24	31.70	6072	138	44.00	293
Croom, L.C.B.	1949	4	8	0	73	26	—	9.12	—	—	—	—
Cross, A.J.	1969	1	2	0	38	20	—	19.00	—	—	—	1
Cross, E.P.	1921–23	7	12	4	61	12*	—	7.62	—	—	—	9/1
Cumbes, J.	1982	14	14	7	33	7*	—	4.71	993	21	47.29	8
Curle, A.C.	1921	3	4	1	60	40	—	20.00	—	—	—	—
Curle, G.	1913	5	9	0	54	34	—	6.00	3	1	—	2
Davies, C.S.	1930–36	8	11	0	112	63	—	10.18	672	14	48.00	3
Davies, R.J.	1976	1	2	0	18	18	—	9.00	—	—	—	1
Dempster, C.S.	1946	3	5	0	69	40	—	13.80	—	—	—	2
Devey, J.H.G.	1894–1907	153	251	20	6515	246	8	28.20	655	16	40.93	67
Dickens, F.	1898–1903	29	32	6	172	35	—	6.61	1782	75	23.76	7
Diver, E.J.	1894–1901	118	186	8	4280	184	4	24.04	187	6	31.16	62/4
Dobson, F.	1928	3	3	0	9	7	—	3.00	138	7	19.71	—
Dobson, K.W.C.	1925	2	4	1	27	12*	—	9.00	24	0	—	—
Docker, L.C.	1894–95	11	18	3	465	85*	—	31.00	—	—	—	8
Dollery, H.E.	1934–55	413	679	63	23457	212	49	38.07	32	0	—	273/13
Dollery, K.R.	1951–56	73	94	21	927	41	—	12.69	5549	215	25.80	16
Donald, A.A.	1987–	18	20	6	185	37*	—	13.21	1541	65	23.78	5
Donnelly, M.P.	1948–50	20	30	0	988	120	1	32.93	35	2	17.50	9
Doshi, D.R.	1980–81	43	45	19	179	35	—	6.88	4649	146	31.84	7
Dunkels, P.R.	1971	1	1	0	0	0	—	—	91	0	—	—
Durnell, T.W.	1921–30	14	13	3	21	5	—	2.10	1190	42	28.33	7
Dyer, R.I.H.B.	1981–86	65	116	11	2843	109*	3	27.07	41	0	—	39
Edmonds, R.B.	1962–67	78	100	31	1006	102*	1	14.57	3994	146	27.35	35
Elson, G	1947	1	2	1	7	4	—	—	116	1	—	—
Everitt, R.S.	1909	3	5	0	57	38	—	11.40	—	—	—	3
Fabling, A.H.	1921	1	2	0	8	7	—	4.00	—	—	—	—
Fantham, W.E.	1935–48	63	103	12	1168	51	—	12.83	2907	64	45.42	34
Farren, G.C.	1912	1	1	0	0	0	—	—	—	—	—	—
Ferreira, A.M.	1979–86	138	194	53	4088	112*	2	28.99	10891	335	32.51	68
Fiddian-Green, C.A.F.	1920–28	64	106	24	2309	95	—	28.15	344	5	68.80	41
Field, E.F.	1897–1920	256	344	102	1867	39	—	7.71	22998	982	23.41	104
Field, M.N.	1974–75	3	1	1	1	1*	—	—	114	0	—	—
Fishwick, T.S.	1896–1909	206	342	13	8644	140*	12	26.27	35	0	—	230/2
Flaherty, K.F.	1969	1	—	—	—	—	—	—	107	4	26.75	—
Fletcher, B.E.	1956–61	49	79	13	1511	102*	1	22.89	13	0	—	39
Flick, B.J.	1969–73	16	14	8	46	18	—	7.66	—	—	—	17/4
Flint, D	1948–49	10	10	3	33	11	—	4.71	465	12	38.75	5
Flower, R.W.	1978	9	8	4	23	10*	—	5.75	554	10	55.40	—
Forrester, T.	1896–99	26	36	13	243	38	—	10.56	2229	77	28.94	14
Foster, A.W.	1914	1	2	1	1	1*	—	—	—	—	—	2
Foster, D.G.	1928–34	52	75	6	728	70	—	10.55	3635	141	25.78	48
Foster, F.R.	1908–14	127	215	14	5436	305*	5	27.04	12069	587	20.56	93
Fox, J.	1922–28	46	50	19	469	27*	—	15.12	908	15	60.53	10
Fox, J.G.	1959–61	43	54	6	515	52	—	10.72	—	—	—	91/14
Franklin, R.C.	1900	1	1	1	0	0*	—	—	—	—	—	1

Name	Seasons	Match	Inns	N.O.	Runs	H.S.	100	Av'ge	Runs	Wts	Av'ge	Ct/st
Gardner, F.C.	1947–61	338	593	66	17826	215*	29	33.82	99	0	—	197
Gardom, B.K.	1973–74	18	25	2	427	79*	—	18.56	700	17	41.17	6
Gaunt, H.C.A.	1919–22	11	20	1	147	32	—	7.73	—	—	—	6
George, W	1901–06	13	18	2	342	71	—	21.37	—	—	—	8
Gibbs, L.R.	1967–72	109	96	48	370	24	—	7.70	8281	338	24.50	80
Gifford, N.	1983–88	139	134	53	741	39	—	9.14	9359	341	27.44	35
Gittins, A.E.	1919	2	3	0	2	2	—	0.66	67	4	16.75	1
Glassford, J.	1969	2	1	0	0	0	—	—	161	5	32.20	1
Glover, A.C.S.	1895–1909	149	226	28	5162	124	7	26.07	1578	49	32.20	81
Glynn, B.T.	1959–61	2	3	1	13	7	—	6.50	—	—	—	1
Gobey, S.C.	1946	2	3	0	2	2	—	0.66	9	0	—	—
Goodway, C.C.	1937–47	40	66	12	434	37*	—	8.03	—	—	—	43/22
Goodwin, H.J.	1907–12	19	36	1	728	101	1	20.80	541	14	38.64	17
Gordon, A	1966–71	34	59	4	891	65	—	16.20	1	0	—	35
Gough-Calthorpe, F.S.	1919–30	231	362	28	8311	209	10	24.88	15299	514	29.76	155
Granville, R. St L.	1934	1	2	0	9	7	—	4.50	—	—	—	—
Gray, J.D.	1968–69	7	6	3	34	18	—	11.33	534	21	25.42	1
Grayland, A.V.	1922–30	4	6	1	15	6*	—	3.00	204	2	102.00	—
Green, J.H.	1927	1	1	1	0	0*	—	—	16	0	—	—
Green, S.J.	1988–	1	2	0	28	28	—	14.00	—	—	—	—
Greening, T.	1912	2	2	1	26	14	—	—	91	1	—	—
Griffiths, S.	1956–58	27	26	12	76	17*	—	5.42	1827	74	24.68	3
Gross, F.A.	1934	1	1	1	0	0*	—	—	76	1	—	1
Grove, C.W.	1938–53	201	288	36	2973	104*	1	11.79	15484	697	22.21	82
Guy, J.B.	1950	2	3	0	24	18	—	8.00	—	—	—	—
Hacking, J.K.	1946	1	2	0	17	14	—	8.50	—	—	—	2
Hall, W	1905	2	3	0	11	8	—	3.66	66	0	—	—
Hampton, W.M.	1922	1	1	0	34	34	—	—	13	0	—	—
Hands, B.O.	1946–47	3	2	0	13	9	—	6.50	137	4	34.25	—
Hands, W.C.	1909–20	60	91	23	856	63	—	12.58	3509	142	24.71	36
Hargreave, S.	1899–1909	188	242	60	1811	45	—	9.95	18496	851	21.73	139
Harris, A.J.	1919	1	2	0	18	14	—	9.00	—	—	—	—
Harris, D.F.	1946	1	1	0	2	2	—	—	—	—	—	—
Harris, E.J.	1975	4	5	2	26	16	—	8.66	295	9	32.77	3
Harris, W.H.	1904–19	12	18	1	204	42	—	12.00	—	—	—	11/2
Hartley, P.J.	1982	3	4	1	31	16	—	10.33	215	2	107.50	1
Harvey, W.H.T.	1927	1	1	0	24	24	—	—	—	—	—	—
Hastilow, C.A.F.	1919	2	3	0	26	14	—	8.66	72	2	36.00	—
Hawkins, C.G.	1957	4	5	2	16	11*	—	5.33	—	—	—	7/2
Hayhurst, A.	1934–35	7	8	0	98	42	—	12.25	457	12	38.08	2
Heath, D.M.W.	1949–53	16	23	1	376	54	—	17.09	—	—	—	7
Hellawell, M.S.	1962	1	2	2	59	30*	—	—	114	6	19.00	—
Hemmings, E.E.	1966–78	177	256	59	4294	85	—	21.79	14056	441	31.87	87
Hewetson, E.P.	1919–27	29	35	7	318	37*	—	11.35	1788	67	26.68	15
Hewitt, E.J.	1954	1	2	0	41	40	—	20.50	60	1	—	—
Hickman, G.	1929	2	4	0	19	17	—	4.75	—	—	—	—
Hilditch, T.A.	1907–13	8	11	1	42	17	—	4.20	319	9	35.44	3
Hill, A.J.B.	1920	1	2	0	4	4	—	2.00	22	0	—	—
Hill, G.H.	1958–60	41	47	6	247	23	—	6.02	3156	107	29.49	25
Hill, H.B.G.	1894–1900	5	7	1	41	13	—	6.83	248	5	49.60	3
Hill, J.E.	1894–98	25	34	4	665	139*	1	22.16	14	0	—	20
Hill, W.A.	1929–48	169	279	22	6423	147*	6	24.99	27	1	—	51
Hitchcock, R.E.	1949–64	319	511	70	12269	153*	13	27.82	5321	182	29.23	110
Hoffman, D.S.	1985	17	15	4	39	13*	—	3.54	1160	29	40.00	3
Hogg, W.	1979–83	50	49	12	279	31	—	7.54	3331	97	34.34	9
Holbech, W.H.	1910	1	2	0	0	0	—	0.00	—	—	—	—
Holdsworth, R.L.	1919–21	30	54	1	1222	141	1	23.05	17	0	—	9
Hollies, W.E.	1932–57	476	570	258	1544	47	—	4.94	45019	2201	20.45	165
Holloway, P.C.L.	1988–	3	5	0	40	16	—	8.00	—	—	—	8/1
Hopkins, D.C.	1977–81	36	44	12	332	34*	—	10.37	2021	53	38.13	8
Hopkins, F.J.	1898–1903	11	16	3	32	13	—	2.46	765	25	30.60	3
Horner, N.F.	1951–65	357	647	33	18217	203*	25	29.66	78	0	—	126
Hossell, J.J.	1939–47	35	62	5	1217	83	—	21.35	370	7	52.85	12

Name	Seasons	Match	Inns	N.O.	Runs	H.S.	100	Av'ge	Runs	Wts	Av'ge	Ct/st
Houghton, W.E.	1946–47	7	11	0	165	41	—	15.00	—	—	—	2
Howell, A.L.	1919–22	34	57	16	249	26	—	6.07	1952	56	34.85	14
Howell, H.	1913–28	198	292	94	1560	36	—	7.87	18089	899	20.12	61
Humpage, G.W.	1974–	309	507	62	16174	254	28	36.34	335	8	41.87	595/68
Hyde, A.J.	1905–07	2	1	1	2	2*	—	—	121	2	60.50	—
Illingworth, E.A.	1920	6	12	3	17	8*	—	1.88	312	8	39.00	2
Jackson, A.K.	1928–31	2	3	2	5	3*	—	5.00	73	0	—	—
Jameson, J.A.	1960–76	343	581	43	18149	240*	31	33.73	3655	83	44.03	242/1
Jameson, T.E.N.	1970	1	2	0	63	32	—	31.50	75	0	—	1
Jarrett, H.H.	1932–33	14	15	1	228	45	—	16.28	1605	47	34.14	5
Jeeves, P.	1912–14	49	80	6	1193	86*	—	16.12	3919	194	20.20	13
Jennings, G.A.	1923–25	20	27	5	243	41	—	11.04	916	23	39.82	8
Jones, A.K.C.	1969–73	4	8	0	176	62	–	22.00	—	—	—	1
Jones, R.H.C.	1946	1	2	0	32	23	—	16.00	27	0	—	1
Kallicharran, A.I.	1971–	262	435	53	17326	243*	50	45.35	2297	47	48.87	161
Kanhai, R.B.	1968–77	173	272	47	11615	253	35	51.62	211	4	52.75	155
Kardar, A.H.	1948–50	45	69	9	1372	112	1	22.86	3183	112	28.41	33
Kemp-Welch, G.D.	1927–35	57	83	7	1419	123*	1	18.67	429	5	85.80	24
Kendall, J.T.	1948–49	4	4	1	26	18*	—	8.66	—	—	—	5/4
Kennedy, J.M.	1960–62	31	55	9	1188	94	—	25.83	1	2	0.50	18
Kent, K.G.	1927–31	9	10	1	40	23*	—	4.44	639	10	63.90	2
Kerr, K.J.	1986	14	12	5	120	45*	—	17.14	955	24	39.79	5
Khalid Ibadulla	1954–72	377	630	69	14766	171	17	26.32	12548	418	30.01	314
Kilner, N.	1924–37	330	539	35	16075	228	23	31.89	166	2	83.00	150
King, E.H.	1928–32	7	10	0	84	24	—	8.40	15	0	—	3
King, I.M.	1952–55	53	60	18	345	29*	—	8.21	2560	95	26.94	31
Kingston, J.P.	1894	1	1	0	24	24	—	—	—	—	—	—
Kinneir, S.P.	1898–1914	302	507	46	15040	268*	25	32.62	1451	48	30.22	179
Kirk, E.	1898	1	1	0	0	0	—	—	—	—	—	1
Kirton, H.O.	1925–29	2	3	0	82	52	—	27.33	—	—	—	—
Knutton, H.J.	1894	1	1	0	4	4	—	—	61	0	—	—
Lane, A.F.	1919–25	12	21	3	259	58	—	14.38	674	23	29.30	7
Langley, C.K.	1908–14	33	52	4	455	61*	—	9.47	1391	54	25.75	12
Latham, H.J.	1955–59	10	13	2	129	26	—	11.72	751	27	27.81	2
Law, A.	1894–99	52	81	5	1459	89	—	19.19	—	—	—	21
Leach, C.W.	1955–58	39	64	6	1025	67	—	17.67	657	26	25.26	28
Leadbeater, E.	1957–58	27	35	5	456	116	1	15.20	1326	52	25.50	18
Legard, E.	1962–68	20	24	11	144	21	—	11.07	—	—	—	33/9
Lethbridge, C.	1981–85	50	58	13	1033	87*	—	22.95	2996	77	38.90	16
Lewington, P.J.	1970–82	69	70	19	376	34	—	7.37	5426	187	29.01	30
Lewis, E.B.	1949–58	43	52	11	541	51	—	13.19	—	—	—	85/22
Lilley, A.F.A.	1894–1911	321	497	29	12813	171	16	27.37	1439	40	35.97	52/132
Lloyd, T.A.	1977–	217	388	33	12626	208*	24	35.56	1142	15	76.13	110
Lobb, B.	1953	1	—	—	—	—	—	—	31	2	15.50	—
Lord, G.J.	1983–86	18	26	2	508	199	1	21.16	37	0	—	6
Lord, W.A.	1897–99	13	18	8	69	10*	—	6.90	811	26	31.19	4
Loveitt, F.R.	1898–1905	25	42	6	846	110	1	23.50	—	—	—	7
Lowe, J.C.M.	1907	1	2	0	8	8	—	4.00	42	1	—	1
Lowe, P.J.	1964	1	—	—	—	—	—	—	—	—	—	2
Luckin, V.V.	1919	9	14	7	195	59*	—	27.85	332	11	30.18	4
Lynes, J.	1898–1905	8	8	0	79	26	—	9.87	576	15	38.40	6
McDowall, J.I.	1969–73	12	21	3	365	89	—	20.27	—	—	—	24/2
McMillan, B.M.	1986	12	21	4	999	136	3	58.76	808	17	47.52	11
McVicker, N.M.	1969–73	104	129	33	1701	65*	—	17.71	7732	300	25.77	30
Manton, J.	1898	1	2	0	5	5	—	2.50	51	1	—	—
Marshall, F.W.	1922	2	2	0	14	10	—	7.00	—	—	—	—
Marshall, G.A.	1961–63	4	5	3	24	18*	—	12.00	221	9	24.55	3
Marshall, J.M.A.	1946–50	28	49	4	790	47	—	17.55	1581	47	33.63	12
Maguire, K.R.	1982	3	3	0	3	2	—	1.00	123	1	—	—

Name	Seasons	Match	Inns	N.O.	Runs	H.S.	100	Av'ge	Runs	Wts	Av'ge	Ct/st
Matheson, E.	1899	1	2	0	14	9	—	7.00	—	—	—	1
Maudsley, R.H.	1946–51	45	74	3	1706	107	2	24.02	1173	39	30.07	33
Mayer, J.H.	1926–39	332	408	115	2832	74*	—	9.66	25356	1142	22.20	182
Maynard, C.	1978–82	24	28	5	550	85	—	23.91	—	—	—	41/5
Mead-Briggs, R.	1946	2	2	1	46	44*	—	—	96	1	—	3
Meldon, W.W.	1909–10	5	9	0	122	44	–	13.55	149	4	37.25	3
Melville, J.	1946	2	3	0	14	13	—	4.66	84	5	16.80	1
Mence, M.D.	1962–65	31	43	8	467	53	—	13.34	1983	61	32.50	16
Merrick, T.A.	1887–	30	40	8	476	74*	—	14.87	2876	122	23.57	11
Meunier, J.B.	1920	2	3	0	12	9	—	4.00	38	0	—	1
Milburn, E.T.	1987	3	4	2	37	24	—	18.50	128	2	64.00	—
Miller, H.R.	1928	1	1	0	8	8	—	—	38	1	—	1
Miller, R.	1961–68	133	166	34	1658	72	—	12.56	7289	241	30.24	144
Mills, J.M.	1946	4	7	0	106	26	—	15.14	167	3	55.66	3
Mitchell, F.R.	1946–48	17	29	2	224	43	—	8.29	856	22	38.90	8
Moles, A.J.	1986–	54	95	9	3137	151	7	36.47	711	17	41.82	41
Monkhouse, S.	1985–86	2	3	1	7	5	—	3.50	95	2	47.50	—
Moorhouse, F.	1900–08	117	154	37	1549	75	—	13.23	6232	260	23.96	54
Morris, L.J.	1925–26	7	11	0	262	76	—	23.81	70	2	23.33	4
Morter, F.W.	1922	3	5	2	13	8	—	4.33	138	3	46.00	—
Morton, J.	1929–30	9	14	0	162	38	—	11.57	—	—	—	4
Morton, W.	1984–85	10	9	2	42	13*	—	6.00	708	16	44.25	6
Munton, T.A.	1985–	52	53	18	305	38	—	8.71	2979	117	2 25.46	
Murray, A.L.	1922	11	17	0	161	33	—	9.47	49	2	24.50	3
Murray, D.L.	1972–75	58	87	12	1773	78	—	23.64	83	0	—	136/15
Myles, S.D.	1988	4	7	0	111	39	—	15.85	65	0	—	—
Nelson, A.L.	1895	1	2	0	0	0	—	0.00	—	—	—	—
Nelson, G.M.B.	1921–22	13	21	8	97	23	—	7.46	746	22	33.90	2
Norton, E.W.	1920	2	1	1	26	26*	—	—	19	0	—	—
Oakes, D.R.	1965	5	8	1	81	33	—	11.57	1	0	—	7
Old, A.G.B.	1969	1	1	0	34	34	—	—	93	1	—	1
Old, C.M.	1983–85	47	53	10	911	70	—	21.18	3596	120	29.96	16
Oliver, P.R.	1975–82	89	128	20	2679	171*	2	24.80	2115	27	78.33	45
Ord, J.S.	1933–53	273	459	35	11788	187*	16	27.80	244	2	122.00	78
O'Rourke, C	1968	1	1	1	23	23*	—	—	—	—	—	3
Paine, G.A.E.	1929–47	240	323	56	3234	79	—	12.11	21867	962	22.73	141
Pallett, H.J.	1894–98	73	98	21	915	55*	—	11.88	6375	296	21.53	20
Palmer, G.A.	1928	9	12	2	87	20	—	8.70	450	8	56.25	7
Parkes, H.R.	1898	1	1	0	1	1	—	—	—	—	—	—
Parry, M.C.	1908–10	2	3	0	26	10	—	8.66	16	0	—	1
Parsons, G.J.	1986–88	47	56	11	918	67*	—	20.40	2961	94	31.50	10
Parsons, J.H.	1910–34	313	494	48	15737	225	35	35.28	1916	55	34.83	207
Partridge, N.E.	1921–37	100	144	17	2352	102	1	18.51	7900	347	22.76	87
Paul, N.A.	1954–55	4	4	0	75	40	—	18.75	65	2	32.50	2
Peare, W.G.	1926	7	9	7	17	12*	—	8.50	75	2	37.50	3
Pell, G.A.	1947	1	2	1	24	16*	—	—	31	4	7.75	1
Pereira, E.J.	1895–96	5	8	1	118	34	—	16.85	13	0	—	2
Perkins, H.G.	1926–27	4	5	2	10	6*	—	3.33	55	1	—	1
Perryman, S.P.	1974–81	131	129	52	745	43	—	9.67	9371	309	30.32	49
Phillips, H.R.	1951	1	1	0	3	3	—	—	—	—	—	—
Phillips, J.H.	1904–11	6	7	0	35	16	—	5.00	159	1	—	5
Pierson, A.R.K.	1985–	25	29	16	192	42*	—	14.76	1312	24	54.66	7
Potter, W.	1932	1	2	0	0	0	—	0.00	31	1	—	1
Pridmore, R.G.	1909–12	14	26	1	315	49	—	12.60	—	—	—	7
Pritchard, T.L.	1946–55	170	247	29	2853	81	—	13.08	16211	695	23.32	68
Pugh, J.G.	1922–27	9	9	0	82	41	—	9.11	206	6	34.33	3
Quaife, B.W.	1920–26	48	81	7	1096	99*	—	14.81	66	4	16.50	11
Quaife, Walter	1894–1901	121	202	11	4935	144	6	25.83	204	7	29.14	45
Quaife, W.G.	1894–1928	665	1112	176	33862	255*	71	36.17	24779	900	27.53	330/1

Name	Seasons	Match	Inns	N.O.	Runs	H.S.	100	Av'ge	Runs	Wts	Av'ge	Ct/st
Ratcliffe, D.P.	1957–58	20	33	2	603	79	—	19.45	—	—	—	18
Ratcliffe, J.D.	1988–	2	4	0	31	16	—	7.75	—	—	—	2
Reeve, D.A.	1988–	16	23	3	431	103	1	21.55	750	24	31.25	11
Rhodes, J.	1895	3	6	0	89	64	—	14.83	—	—	—	2
Rhodes, T.B.	1899	4	7	1	105	55	—	17.50	—	—	—	3
Rice, W.I.	1920	2	4	0	15	9	—	3.75	—	—	—	1
Richards, W.	1895–96	7	11	1	112	61*	—	11.20	—	—	—	4
Richardson, B.A.	1963–67	40	72	4	1323	126	2	19.45	153	1	—	28
Richardson, S.H.	1920	2	4	1	18	8*	—	6.00	—	—	—	—
Riley, T.M.N.	1961–64	12	23	2	440	84	—	20.95	15	0	—	2
Roberts, H.E.	1949–50	5	8	0	52	30	—	6.50	—	—	—	3
Roberts, H.J.	1932–37	17	27	4	348	61	—	15.13	407	9	45.22	11
Robins, D.H.	1947	2	4	1	54	29*	—	18.00	—	—	—	3
Robinson, M.	1951–52	8	13	1	234	57	—	19.50	5	0	—	1
Robinson, T.L.	1946	4	7	1	27	13*	—	4.50	277	6	46.16	—
Roll, H.	1927	1	1	0	0	0	—	0.00	40	0	—	1
Rotherham, G.A.	1919–21	44	75	4	1061	62	—	14.94	3678	130	28.29	36
Rotherham, H.	1903	1	1	0	33	33	—	—	—	—	—	2
Rouse, S.J.	1970–81	124	152	33	1862	93	—	15.64	8043	266	30.23	53
Russell, J.B.	1920	1	2	0	31	23	—	15.50	—	—	—	1/1
Sale, R.	1939–47	19	33	3	929	157	2	30.96	—	—	—	2
Sanders, W.	1928–34	84	100	18	706	64	—	8.60	4663	119	39.18	46
Sanderson, G.B.	1901	1	1	0	0	0	—	—	—	—	—	—
Santall, F.R.	1919–39	496	789	84	17518	201*	21	24.84	12186	280	43.52	267
Santall, S.	1894–1914	370	534	117	6490	73	—	15.56	28923	1207	23.96	161
Savage, R. le Q.	1976–79	23	23	14	67	15*	—	7.44	1924	54	35.62	8
Scorer, R.I.	1921–26	29	52	8	718	113	1	16.31	659	18	36.61	10
Sharp, N.	1923	1	1	0	3	3	—	—	—	—	—	1
Shaw, D.G.	1949	1	1	0	17	17	—	—	106	2	53.00	—
Shilton, J.E.	1894–95	19	23	6	152	30	—	8.94	1300	56	3.21	12
Shortland, N.A.	1938–50	23	40	5	487	70	—	13.91	50	0	—	4
Shuckburgh, C.G.S.	1930	1	1	0	0	0	—	—	—	—	—	1
Simms, H.L.	1921–22	5	10	0	133	38	—	13.30	216	5	43.20	1
Small, G.C.	1980–	163	205	42	2386	70	—	14.63	12720	462	27.53	47
Smart, C.C.	1920–22	45	81	10	922	59	—	12.98	508	9	56.44	40
Smart, J.A.	1919–36	238	340	43	3425	68*	—	11.53	1262	22	57.36	317/105
Smith, A.C.	1958–74	358	499	74	8452	94	—	19.88	2894	118	24.52	589/39
Smith, D.M.	1981–83	4	5	2	148	100*	1	49.33	191	2	95.50	2
Smith, E.J.	1904–30	444	744	48	15911	177	20	22.86	81	1	—	665/138
Smith, I.W.	1905	1	1	0	1	1	—	—	13	0	—	—
Smith, K.D.	1973–85	196	346	28	8718	140	9	27.42	3	0	—	70
Smith, M.J.K.	1956–75	430	741	99	27672	200*	48	43.10	112	3	37.33	422
Smith, N.M.K.	1987–	3	5	1	59	23	—	14.75	172	4	43.00	1
Smith, P.A.	1982–	128	213	24	5252	119	2	27.78	5428	130	41.75	39
Smith, W.J.	1906	1	1	0	0	0	—	—	93	2	46.50	—
Speed, A.W.	1927–28	8	7	3	29	11*	—	7.25	538	29	18.55	1
Spencer, H.N.E.	1930	3	2	1	4	3*	—	2.00	146	1	—	1
Spooner, R.T.	1948–59	312	506	59	12014	168	11	26.87	11	0	—	527/155
Stephens, F.G.	1907–12	32	50	7	1102	144*	1	25.62	205	3	68.33	17
Stephens, G.W.	1907–25	123	203	13	3997	143	3	21.03	80	4	20.00	46
Stevenson, J.F.	1919	1	2	0	18	18	—	9.00	—	—	—	—
Stewart, W.J.P.	1955–69	279	471	53	14249	182*	25	34.08	15	2	7.50	128
Storie, A.C.	1987–88	25	43	10	665	68	—	20.15	20	0	—	22
Street, L.C.	1946	4	7	2	17	8*	—	3.40	146	3	48.66	2
Street, N.K.	1908	5	9	0	43	14	—	4.77	—	—	—	3
Suckling, E.	1919	2	3	0	45	39	—	15.00	29	0	—	—
Sutcliffe, S.P.	1981–83	20	21	8	57	20	—	4.38	2475	46	53.80	3
Swaranjit Singh	1956–58	27	43	10	872	68*	—	26.42	1248	42	29.71	12
Tate, C.F.	1931–33	7	8	2	34	17	—	5.66	297	6	49.50	5
Tayler, F.E.	1910	4	8	0	112	44	—	14.00	5	0	—	—
Taylor, A.	1913	6	11	2	83	17	—	9.22	137	4	34.25	3
Taylor, A.E.	1927	1	1	0	0	0	—	—	7	0	—	—

Name	Seasons	Match	Inns	N.O.	Runs	H.S.	100	Av'ge	Runs	Wts	Av'ge	Ct/st
Taylor, C.J.	1908–09	3	4	0	6	5	—	1.50	257	9	28.55	1
Taylor, C.R.V.	1970	1	—	—	—	—	—	—	—	—	—	2
Taylor, D.D.S.	1948–50	16	23	7	519	121	1	32.43	607	15	40.46	4
Taylor, D.D.	1949–53	45	82	5	1624	90*	—	21.09	246	11	22.36	25
Taylor, F.	1939	1	1	0	0	0	—	—	71	3	23.66	1
Taylor, K.A.	1946–49	87	155	10	3145	102	1	21.68	33	1	—	42
Tedstone, G.A.	1982–88	32	44	6	641	67*	—	16.86	—	—	—	49/10
Tennant, P.N.	1964	1	—	—	—	—	—	—	—	—	—	3/1
Thomas, G.P.	1978–81	8	15	1	277	52	—	19.78	—	—	—	6
Thompson, J.R.	1938–54	44	76	3	1922	103	2	26.32	13	0	—	15
Thompson, R.G.	1949–62	158	185	70	655	25*	—	5.69	10824	472	22.93	51
Tidy, W.N.	1970–74	36	34	14	70	12*	—	3.50	2775	81	34.25	17
Timms, B.S.V.	1969–71	24	33	7	421	61	—	16.19	—	—	—	54/10
Thorne, D.A.	1983–	38	60	9	940	76	—	18.43	452	3	150.66	32
Townsend, A.	1948–60	340	549	69	11965	154	6	24.92	9238	323	28.60	409
Tudor, R.T.	1976	1	1	0	6	6	—	—	42	0	—	—
Venn, H.	1919–25	34	60	0	1047	151	2	17.45	28	0	—	14
Waddy, E.F.	1919–22	26	42	2	955	109*	1	23.87	—	—	—	15
Walker, G.	1912	1	2	0	13	13	—	6.50	—	—	—	—
Wall, S.	1984–85	19	25	9	175	28	—	10.93	1522	37	41.13	6
Ward, L.M.	1930	1	1	0	5	5	—	5.00	29	1	—	1
Ward, W.	1895–1904	11	16	5	79	26	—	7.18	965	30	32.16	3
Waring, J.S.	1967	1	2	0	15	15	—	7.50	129	2	64.50	—
Warner, G.S.	1966–71	30	48	7	965	118*	2	23.53	14	0	—	13
Wassall, A.	1923	7	11	3	24	10	—	3.00	344	10	34.40	4
Watson, T.H.	1904	2	3	0	18	12	—	6.00	137	0	—	—
Watson, Smith, H.	1912	1	1	0	15	15	—	—	—	—	—	—
Webster, R.V.	1962–66	60	66	15	658	47	—	12.90	4532	234	19.36	16
Weeks, R.T.	1950–57	105	139	35	1047	51	—	10.06	6004	228	26.33	41
Weldrick, G.	1906–07	8	11	1	53	12	—	5.30	—	—	—	3
Welford, J.W.	1896	13	23	2	459	118	1	21.85	180	2	90.00	2
Wheatley, O.S.	1957–60	63	76	34	207	17	—	4.92	5971	237	25.19	19
White, A.F.T.	1936–37	9	15	2	311	55*	—	23.92	—	—	—	4
White, H.A.	1923	8	15	3	107	32	—	8.91	33	0	—	2
White, M.F.	1946	1	2	0	0	0	—	0.00	—	—	—	3/1
Whitehead, J.G.	1902	1	1	0	1	1	—	—	50	0	—	1
Whitehead, S.J.	1894–1900	55	74	26	463	46*	—	9.64	4018	170	23.63	32
Whitehouse, J.	1971–80	179	307	38	8689	197	15	32.30	471	6	78.50	120
Whitehouse, P.G.	1926	3	6	3	41	13	—	13.66	122	8	15.25	6
Whittle, A.E.M.	1900–06	60	80	10	1685	104	1	24.07	2011	56	35.91	31
Williams, O.L.	1967	1	2	1	6	6	—	—	60	1	—	—
Williams, R.P.	1897–98	5	8	1	80	38	—	11.42	14	0	—	7
Willis, R.G.D.	1972–84	136	138	55	1389	43	—	16.73	8769	353	24.84	55
Wilmot, K.	1931–39	75	101	25	871	54	—	11.46	5018	154	32.58	23
Wilson, B.A.	1951	1	1	0	0	0	—	—	75	1	—	—
Windridge, J.E.	1909–13	7	12	1	161	34*	—	14.63	13	1	—	2
Wolton, A.V.G.	1947–60	296	477	61	12896	165	12	31.00	1226	37	33.13	117
Woodroffe, A.	1947–48	4	7	0	77	41	—	11.00	—	—	—	3
Wootton, S.H.	1981–83	11	16	2	364	104	1	26.00	7	0	—	4
Wright, A.	1960–64	76	76	27	315	27	—	6.42	5953	236	25.22	29
Wyatt, R.E.S.	1923–39	404	627	105	21687	232	51	41.55	21401	652	32.83	231
Youll, M.	1956–57	4	2	0	15	9	—	7.50	302	14	21.57	—

Gillette Cup and
Nat-West Trophy Career Records

Name	Years	Match	Inns	N.O.	Runs	H.S.	Av'ge	Ct	Runs	100	Wts	Av'ge
Abberley, R.N.	1966–78	14	13	2	128	47	16.18	2	—	—	—	—
Amiss, D.L.	1963–87	57	55	9	1950	135	39.00	5	67	2	—	—
Asif Din, M.	1981–	15	13	4	221	45	24.55	—	5	—	1	5.00
Bannister, J.D.	1963–68	15	7	4	10	4	3.33	1	428	—	19	22.52
Barber, R.W.	1963–69	18	18	1	652	114	38.35	5	117	2	5	23.40
Blenkiron, W.	1965–74	9	7	2	66	22	13.20	4	331	—	18	18.38
Bourne, W.A.	1975–77	5	3	1	16	9	8.00	—	211	—	5	42.20
Brown, D.J.	1964–79	32	17	5	160	41	13.33	4	1066	—	51	20.90
Cartwright, T.W.	1963–69	17	13	2	108	37	9.81	5	477	—	22	21.68
Claughton, J.A.	1980	2	2	1	23	23	23.00	1	5	—	—	—
Doshi, D.R.	1980	3	—	—	—	—	—	—	98	—	6	16.33
Donald, A.A.	1987–	3	—	—	—	—	—	1	88	—	10	8.80
Dyer, R.I.H.B.	1983–85	7	7	—	205	119	29.28	2	—	1	—	—
Edmonds, R.B.	1965–66	3	1	1	12	12*	—	1	73	—	7	10.42
Ferreira, A.M.	1979–86	17	13	6	166	32*	23.71	7	565	—	28	20.17
Gifford, N.	1983–88	16	7	4	22	6*	7.33	1	398	—	22	18.09
Gibbs, L.R.	1968–72	12	5	4	20	6*	20.00	7	396	—	14	28.28
Green, S.J.	1988	1	1	—	1	1	1.00	—	—	—	—	—
Hemmings, E.E.	1970–78	9	7	1	69	20	11.50	2	387	—	9	43.00
Hitchcock, R.E.	1963–64	5	5	2	91	47*	30.33	1	69	—	5	13.80
Hogg, W.	1981–83	3	2	1	13	9*	13.00	—	146	—	2	73.00
Hopkins, D.C.	1979–80	3	1	—	2	2	2.00	—	85	—	5	17.00
Horner, N.F.	1963–64	5	5	1	125	55	31.25	—	—	—	—	—
Humpage, G.W.	1976–	31	29	4	720	76	28.80	32/6	—	—	—	—
Jameson, J.A.	1963–76	32	31	2	758	100*	26.13	11	138	1	6	23.00
Kallicharran, A.I.	1972	26	25	2	1169	206	50.86	13	319	3	14	22.78
Kanhai, R.B.	1968–77	20	20	3	739	126	43.47	13	—	1	—	—
Khalid Ibadulla	1963–71	22	22	3	440	75	23.15	4	723	—	42	17.21
Lloyd, T.A.	1978	23	23	3	897	121	44.55	7	47	1	2	23.50
McVicker, N.W.	1969–73	11	9	2	73	42	10.42	2	421	—	16	26.31
Merrick, T.A.	1988–	2	2	—	15	13	7.50	—	39	—	3	13.00
Mence, M.D.	1963	1	1	1	11	11	—	—	29	—	—	—
Moles, A.J.	1986–	6	6	—	179	127	29.83	1	81	1	—	—
Murray, D.L.	1972–75	7	6	2	137	76*	34.25	10	—	—	—	—
Munton, T.A.	1987–	3	1	1	0	0*	—	—	105	—	2	52.50
Oliver, P.R.	1976–82	14	10	5	99	32*	19.80	2	261	—	3	87.00
Parsons, G.J.	1986–88	7	6	2	51	19	12.75	1	204	—	6	34.00
Perryman, S.P.	1975–79	6	3	2	8	4*	8.00	1	234	—	9	26.00
Reeve, D.A.	1988–	1	1	—	13	13	13.00	—	2	—	—	—
Richardson, B.A.	1964	1	1	—	17	17	17.00	—	—	—	—	—
Rouse, S.J.	1971–81	16	9	2	74	34	10.56	2	653	—	21	31.09
Small, G.C.	1980–	18	11	5	104	33	17.33	—	4	605	23	26.30
Smith, A.C.	1963–74	25	19	5	262	39*	18.71	—	32	63	—	—
Smith, K.D.	1978–84	16	16	1	609	113	40.60	2	3	—	—	—
Smith, M.J.K.	1964–75	27	26	3	791	88*	34.39	—	13	8	—	—
Stewart, W.J.	1964–69	14	13	1	253	59	21.08	—	2	—	—	—
Storie, A.C.	1987–88	4	4	2	45	25*	22.50	—	—	—	—	—
Sutcliffe, S.P.	1982	2	—	—	—	—	—	—	2	67	5	13.40
Snow, J.A.	1980	1	1	—	13	13	13.00	—	—33	—	—	—
Tedstone, G.A.	1987–88	1	1	1	55	55*	—	—	—	—	—	—

Name	Seasons	Match	Inns	N.O.	Runs	H.S.	100	Av'ge	Runs	Wts	Av'ge	Ct/st
Thorne, D.A.	1984–	4	4	—70	21	12.50	—	—	—	—	—	
Webster, R.V.	1964–66	6	2	—	22	11	11.00	—	2	164	4	41.00
Whitehouse, J.	1971–80	14	14	1	538	109	47.38	1	1	—	—	—
Willis, R.G.D.	1972–84	26	9	5	27	8*	6.75	—	4	753	43	17.51
Wootton, S.H.	1981	1	1	—	2	2	2.00	—	—	—	—	—
Wright, A.	1963–64	2	1	—	12	12	12.00	—	—	51	1	51.00

Benson & Hedges Cup Career Records

Name	Years	Match	Inns	N.O.	Runs	H.S.	100	Av'ge	Ct	Runs	Wts	Av'ge
Abberley, R.N.	1972–79	19	18	3	509	113*	1	33.93	7	30	1	30.00
Amiss, D.L.	1972–87	75	67	7	2092	115	2	34.86	18	4	—	—
Asif Din, M.	1981–	26	23	4	598	107	1	31.47	2	62	1	62.00
Blenkiron, W.	1972–74	4	2	—	7	5	—	3.50	—	138	4	34.50
Bourne, W.	1975–77	17	9	4	88	34	—	17.60	9	626	27	23.18
Brown, D.J.	1972–79	39	13	6	83	20*	—	11.85	3	1184	43	27.53
Claughton, J.A.	1980	4	4	—	131	52	—	32.75	—	—	—	—
Cumbes, J.	1982	4	2	1	1	1*	—	1.00	4	159	5	31.80
Donald, A.A.	1987–	3	1	—	0	0	—	—	1	91	7	13.00
Doshi, D.R.	1980–81	5	3	3	20	19*	—	—	—	218	3	76.66
Dyer, R.I.H.B.	1984–86	9	9	—	142	54	—	15.77	1	—	—	—
Ferreira, A.M.	1979–85	31	24	8	393	71	—	24.56	4	1318	47	28.04
Gibbs, L.R.	1972–73	9	3	1	5	4	—	2.50	2	294	13	22.61
Gifford, N.	1983–88	24	9	5	17	8	—	4.25	3	832	26	32.00
Hemmings, E.E.	1973–78	26	14	4	185	61*	—	18.50	9	842	25	33.68
Hogg, W.	1981–83	10	4	—	9	5	—	2.25	3	325	12	27.08
Humpage, G.W.	1976–	62	55	7	1309	100*	—	27.27	67/3	123	3	42.00
Jameson, J.A.	1972–76	25	25	—	580	94	—	23.20	12	135	6	22.50
Kallicharran, A.I.	1972–	60	56	7	2140	122*	4	43.67	16	111	—	—
Kanhai, R.B.	1972–77	31	30	13	1073	119*	2	63.11	16	—	—	—
Khalid Ibadulla	1972	4	2	1	33	25	—	33.00	1	—	—	—
Lethbridge, C.	1982–85	11	6	2	34	13*	—	8.50	2	337	10	33.70
Lloyd, T.A.	1978–	40	37	3	1153	137*	1	33.91	8	76	—	—
Lord, G.J.	1986	1	1	—	0	0	—	—	—	—	—	—
Maynard, C.	1979–81	3	3	1	26	17*	—	13.00	3	—	—	—
McMillan, B.M.	1986	4	4	—	170	76	–	42.50	2	161	6	26.83
McVicker, N.M.	1972–73	10	4	1	38	23	—	12.66	2	292	19	15.36
Merrick, T.A.	1987–	6	4	1	27	18*	—	9.00	1	127	5	25.40
Moles, A.J.	1987–	9	8	—	228	72	—	28.50	1	115	2	57.50
Munton, T.A.	1986–	7	4	4	9	6*	—	—	2	254	7	36.28
Murray, D.L.	1972–75	20	15	5	303	82	—	30.30	19/2	—	—	—
Old, C.M.	1983–85	12	7	2	153	57	—	30.60	1	430	13	33.07
Oliver, P.R.	1976–82	19	18	3	276	46	—	18.40	5	—	—	—
Parsons, G.J.	1986–88	11	8	2	61	20	—	10.16	3	347	10	34.70
Perryman, S.P.	1975–81	30	10	7	30	18	—	10.00	5	979	34	28.40
Pierson, A.K.	1985–	4	4	2	18	11	—	9.00	1	122	5	24.40
Reeve, D.A.	1988–	5	5	3	49	20*	—	24.50	—	98	2	49.00
Rouse, S.J.	1972–81	35	15	5	144	34*	—	14.40	4	1109	58	19.12
Savage, R.L.Q.	1979	1	1	1	1	1*	—	—	—	46	—	—
Small, G.C.	1980–	32	19	5	79	19*	—	5.64	7	1053	34	30.97
Smith, A.C.	1973–74	5	1	—	8	8	—	8.00	—	122	3	40.66
Smith, K.D.	1977–85	32	29	2	1020	84	—	37.77	4	—	—	—
Smith, M.J.K.	1972–75	19	18	3	367	62*	—	24.46	4	—	—	—
Smith, P.A.	1982–	23	21	3	299	43	—	16.61	4	342	10	34.20
Sutcliffe, S.P.	1982	1	—	—	—	—	—	—	—	55	—	—
Storrie, A.C.	1987–88	4	3	—	142	66	—	47.33	2	—	—	—
Tedstone, G.A.	1988	7	1	—	—	—	—	—	—	—	—	—
Thorne, D.A.	1987–	4	3	1	47	30	—	23.50	—	21	—	—
Wall, S.	1985	4	1	—	6	6	—	6.00	3	141	3	47.00
Whitehouse, J.	1972–79	27	25	2	710	71*	—	30.87	10	—	—	—
Willis, R.G.D.	1973–84	50	18	2	133	37	—	8.31	15	1505	87	17.29
Wootton, S.H.	1983	1	1	—	33	33	—	33.00	1	—	—	—

Sunday League Career Records

Name	Years	Match	Inns	N.O.	Runs	H.S.	Av'ge	100	Ct	Runs	Wts	Av'ge
Abberley, R.N.	1969–79	97	89	5	1647	76	19.60	—	24	353	10	35.30
Amiss, D.L.	1969–87	244	239	20	7040	117*	32.14	5	70	23	1	23.00
Asif Din, M.	1981	102	89	15	1881	108*	25.41	1	16	90	3	30.00
Banks, D.A.	1988–	5	5	1	128	51*	32.00	—	1	—	—	—
Bannister, J.D.	1969	3	1	1	0	0*	—	—	2	71	4	17.75
Barber, R.W.	1969–71	17	17	—	262	46	15.41	—	2	—	—	—
Blenkiron, W.	1969–74	64	45	8	326	51	8.81	—	14	1986	86	23.09
Bourne, W.A.	1974–77	46	31	6	233	33*	9.32	—	15	1474	51	28.90
Brown, D.J.	1969–79	109	63	20	447	38*	10.39	—	19	3288	123	26.73
Bulpitt, N.J.	1979	3	2	—	18	11	9.00	—	—	107	2	53.50
Cartwright, T.W.	1969	11	8	—	128	41	16.00	—	4	246	22	11.18
Claughton, J.A.	1980	12	11	1	213	65	21.30	—	5	—	—	—
Clifford, C.C.	1979	3	3	2	4	2*	4.00	—	—	114	5	22.80
Cumbes, J.	1982	8	3	1	19	14*	9.50	—	1	222	6	37.00
Donald, A.A.	1987–	9	7	4	48	18*	16.00	—	3	296	12	24.67
Doshi, D.R.	1980	14	2	—	9	6	4.50	—	2	425	21	20.23
Dyer, R.I.H.B.	1982–85	26	22	2	357	50	17.85	—	7	21	—	—
Ferreira, A.M.	1979–86	93	70	18	1217	52	23.40	—	15	3264	124	26.32
Field, M.N.	1974	5	1	1	0	0*	—	—	—	131	2	65.50
Flick, B.J.	1971–73	6	4	3	7	4*	7.00	—	2	—	—	—
Gardom, B.K.	1973–74	5	3	—	2	2	0.66	—	—	2	—	—
Green, S.J.	1988–	3	3	1	11	10*	5.50	—	—	—	—	—
Gibbs, L.R.	1969–73	26	15	5	27	8*	2.70	—	7	778	33	23.57
Gifford, N.	1983–88	75	24	15	170	32*	18.88	—	15	2260	82	27.56
Gordon, A.	1970–71	4	3	—	38	21	12.66	—	—	—	—	—
Hartley, P.J.	1982	1	—	—	—	—	—	—	—	19	—	—
Hemmings, E.E.	1969–78	102	76	16	745	44*	12.41	—	37	3087	108	28.58
Hodgson, G.D.	1987	1	1	—	12	12	12.00	—	1	—	—	—
Hoffman, D.S.	1985	9	3	2	3	2	3.00	—	1	252	5	50.40
Hogg, W.	1981–83	25	6	3	20	9*	6.66	—	5	807	20	40.35
Holloway, P.C.L.	1988–	2	2	—	20	13	20.00	—	1	—	—	—
Hopkins, D.C.	1978–80	21	10	3	58	35*	8.28	—	3	627	17	36.88
Humpage, G.W.	1975–	184	171	24	3802	109*	25.86	2	116/20	556	15	37.06
Jameson, J.A.	1969–76	111	108	6	3077	123*	30.16	5	38	477	24	19.87
Jones, A.K.C.	1973	3	3	1	28	21	14.00	—	1	—	—	—
Kallicharran, A.I.	1972–	170	160	18	4340	102*	30.56	4	30	880	14	62.85
Kanhai, R.	1969–77	91	87	11	2631	120	34.61	4	36	2	1	2.00
Kerr, K.J.	1986	7	4	2	9	5*	4.50	—	—	156	4	39.00
Khalid Ibadulla	1969–72	33	28	2	299	29	11.50	—	8	977	34	28.73
Lethbridge, C.	1981–85	37	20	12	210	57*	26.25	—	13	1250	39	32.50
Lewington, P.J.	1971–73	2	1	1	0	0*	—	—	—	71	2	35.50
Lloyd, T.A.	1976–	128	123	12	3263	90	29.39	—	26	149	1	—
Lord, G.J.	1983–86	12	12	1	243	103	22.09	1	4	—	—	—
McDowall, J.I.	1973	2	1	—	1	1	1.00	—	4	—	—	—
McMillan, B.M.	1986	5	5	2	133	78*	44.33	—	3	177	7	25.28
McVicker, N.M.	1969–73	65	44	15	474	45	16.34	—	6	1966	86	22.86
Maguire, R.K.	1982	2	1	—	0	0	—	—	1	85	1	85.00
Maynard, C.	1978–81	30	25	7	282	35	15.66	—	24/2	—	—	—
Merrick, T.A.	1987–	16	8	1	104	59	14.86	—	2	458	20	22.90
Moles, A.J.	1986–	29	27	2	577	85	23.08	—	8	358	7	51.14
Morton, W.	1984	1	1	—	10	10	10.00	—	—	25	—	—
Munton, T.A.	1986–	32	8	6	23	7*	11.50	—	1	909	31	29.32

Name	Years	match	Inns	N.O.	Runs	H.S.	Av'ge	100	Ct	Runs	Wts	Av'ge
Murray, D.L.	1972–75	47	38	12	585	65*	22.50	—	39/4	—	—	—
Myles, S.D.	1988	2	1	—	32	32	32.00	—	—	—	—	—
Old, C.M.	1983–85	24	14	3	283	58	25.72	—	2	721	20	23.05
Oliver, P.R.	1975–82	79	70	16	1323	78*	24.50	—	20	1328	42	31.61
Parsons, G.J.	1986–88	25	17	7	156	26*	15.60	—	4	709	23	30.83
Perryman, S.P.	1975–81	73	26	18	70	17*	8.75	—	17	2270	68	33.38
Pierson, A.R.K.	1985–	22	12	6	61	21*	10.16	—	12	604	10	60.40
Reeve, D.A.	1988–	12	10	3	225	69	32.14	—	5	359	18	19.94
Rouse, S.J.	1970–81	112	68	23	491	38*	10.91	—	25	3521	110	32.00
Sam, C.A.	1979	2	2	—	32	31	16.00	—	1	—	—	—
Savage, RleQ	1976–79	11	3	1	1	1*	1.00	—	1	420	12	35.00
Small, G.C.	1980–	95	50	17	258	40*	7.82	—	18	3107	141	22.04
Smith, A.C.	1969–74	49	38	12	298	36*	11.46	—	23/2	455	16	28.43
Smith, K.D.	1975–84	59	57	3	1136	73	21.03	—	11	—	—	—
Smith, M.J.K.	1969–75	92	85	11	1944	97*	26.27	—	22	—	—	—
Smith, N.M.K.	1987–	7	4	—	27	22	6.75	—	2	64	1	64.00
Smith, P.A.	1982–	78	68	18	1079	56	21.58	—	15	1638	50	32.76
Snow, J.A.	1980	6	4	4	44	25*	—	—	—	204	8	25.50
Stewart, W.J.	1969	5	5	1	65	27	16.25	—	—	—	—	—
Storie, A.C.	1987–88	5	4	—	86	55	21.50	—	2	—	—	—
Sutcliffe, S.P.	1982	3	—	—	—	—	—	—	—	146	3	48.66
Tedstone, G.A.	1982–88	10	5	2	74	31*	24.66	—	10/2	—	—	—
Thomas, G.P.	1978	1	1	—	16	16	—	—	—	—	—	—
Thorne, D.A.	1983–	34	29	10	409	59*	21.53	—	7	580	13	44.61
Tidy, W.H.	1970	1	—	—	—	—	—	—	—	37	3	12.33
Timms, B.S.V.	1969–70	7	5	3	34	29	17.00	—	4/1	—	—	—
Wall, S.	1984–85	6	2	1	8	6	8.00	—	—	195	4	48.75
Warner, G.S.	1969–71	9	8	—	83	39	10.37	—	3	—	—	—
Whitehouse, J.	1971–80	103	98	8	1858	92	20.64	—	32	36	1	36.00
Willis, R.G.D.	1972–84	109	44	20	259	52*	10.79	—	31	3154	144	21.90
Wootton, S.H.	1981–83	13	10	4	135	28*	22.50	—	3	—	—	—

Afterword by Andy Lloyd

During my time at Edgbaston it has been my privilege to play alongside some of the great names of Warwickshire cricket. These men are familiar to you all and their contributions to the club are in the record books for all to see. However, cricket is a team game and some lesser-known players have also made a mark on me, not so much for their performances on the field but for their personality off it.

Many people recognize the fact that team spirit is an important ingredient in all team games. In this marvellous production the facts and figures tell one part of the cricketer's story but do not ignore the fact that this immeasurable quality may also have helped win a game or two. It is often not the stars but the day-in day-out county players who contribute most towards that end in cricket.

We will all use the book as a form of reference, and I have no doubt that old cricketing arguments can be settled. Who scored most runs, who took most wickets and who played most matches will all be answered in a second, and I am sure all followers of Warwickshire will find the book illuminating. Being anything but a statistician myself, I will obviously be brushing up on my own cricketing knowledge.

As present-day captain of Warwickshire, nobody is more aware than I of the luck that is involved in winning matches and indeed trophies. In my memory our team of the early seventies was exceptional, but I'm sure even that side can look back on times of good fortune. But whilst luck is something you cannot measure, put that along with a good team and a trophy is never far away.

In this book cricketing fortunes of all types are gathered together, and of one thing I'm sure: there is a new fact for everyone to learn, somewhere in the foregoing pages.

Subscribers

Warwickshire County
    Cricket Club
Brooke, Robert
Goodyear, David
Adkins, E.F.
Allen, Heather
Amiss, Dennis L.
Bailey, Philip
Blakemore, David B.
Blogg, J.R.
Bolton, Paul
Booth, Frank
Bourne, Leonard R.T.
Bridgman, J.M.
Brueton, Stephen
Bryant, David C.
Cartwright, Simon J.
Claughton, R.K.
Coleman, Rick (The Pro)
Colquhoun, Andy
Cook, Keith
Cookson, Michael
Cooper, Bryan Robert
Cooper, Josephine
Cunnington, Glenys
Davis, Alex E.
Derricott, D.J.
Duckett, John
Dutton, Eric
Dyer MBE, Major I.C.
Dyer, R.I.H.B.
Eagle, B.E.
Evans, David
Evans, W.B.
Fellows, L.F.
Ferreira, Anton
Finglas, Christopher
Fisher, Francis
Fisher, Nicholas
Gent, R.F.
Gerald (TVR Ltd), David

Glover, Margaret
Goodway, C.C.
Goodyear, William B.
Goulden, M.
Graham, Kenneth William
Green, Jennifer
Gross, Nicholas Clive
Harvey, G.A.
Higgs, Renee
Hodder, Brian (The Owl)
Holbech, Geoffrey
Houlder, I.M.
Huband, John
Hudson, John
Hunt, Brian
Hunt, D.
Hunt, Ray
Hurst, M.
James, R.
Jameson, John A.
Johnson, Dennis H.
Jones, Maurice
Jones, V.J.
Knibb, T.J.
Lee, A.D.
Lee, D.B.
Locke, M.J.C.
Long, Richard
Lythall, G.H.
Marcuson, S.
Mills, Roger J.
Moles, A.J.
Moore, Ray T.
Myles, R.K.
Parker, John
Peakman, K.J.
Penney, I.A.
Perkins, Brian Kenneth
Peter, M.A.
Pickering, Ian Jack
Pountney, C.

Powell, Glyn
Power, Alan Edward
Preece, D.
Price, Charles W.
Prince, F.
Ratcliffe, David P.
Redshaw, C.
Reeves, John
Reeves, Keith Neil
Rippon, Anton
Roberts, B.S.
Roberts, David H.
Salmon, L.E.
Senior, Darren
Shannon, Philip
Shaw, John (The Orgy)
Sheen, Steve
Skett, Paul
Smith, M.J.K.
Stanford, B.A.
Stanley, John
Steer, Gary
Stretton, Neil
Taylor, A.J.
Thomas, G.
Townsend, Alan
Townsend, J.
Tyreman, G.V.
Tyson, C.E.
Vale, Simon
Walls, J.
Walton, Tim
Warwick, T.
Watton, Harry
Weedon, David B.
Wilkinson, David
Williams, Steve
Wolton, A.V.
Woodward, John
Wright, Adrian J.
Wright, R.W.